Biblical Resources for Ministry

David R. Bauer

**A BIBLIOGRAPHY
OF WORKS
IN BIBLICAL STUDIES**

Second Edition,
Revised and Enlarged

 **Evangel Publishing House**
2000 Evangel Way - P.O. Box 189
Nappanee, Indiana 46550

Cover Design: Barbara Thompson

ISBN: 0-916035-62-X

Library of Congress Catalog Card Number: 95-61365

Printed in the United States of America

5 4 3 2 1

This book is dedicated to

my students

who give to me joy in teaching

TABLE OF CONTENTS

THE INTERTESTAMENTAL PERIOD

THE NEW TESTAMENT

INTRODUCTION

The interpretation of the Bible is a central concern to all Christian ministers; for integrity demands that all ministers, in whatever capacity they serve, be professionally informed and personally shaped by the message of the Scriptures. The interpretation of the Bible involves, first of all, direct, first-hand study of the text. But it must also include, at the proper time, the use of various kinds of secondary sources. These resources are the indispensable tools of the biblical interpreter.

I have compiled the following bibliography with these considerations in mind. Although this book includes approximately fifteen hundred titles by nine hundred scholars, it is still a highly selective bibliography, containing only a fraction of works that could have been included. Inclusion of individual items was based upon one or more of the following considerations: (1) usefulness for the theological interpretation of the Bible within the context of the faith of the church; (2) significance in the history of interpretation; and (3) representation of evangelical and especially evangelical Wesleyan scholarship. I have marked with an asterisk (*) those items deemed most helpful.

I readily concede that any attempt to develop a bibliography and to identify within that bibliography works that deserve special attention is a matter of individual judgment; no two scholars would agree on the selection. Thus, I present this bibliography as a suggestion, a place to start, inviting students to test the worth of these items in the process of the interpretive task.

I have prepared this volume for use primarily by seminary students and ministers. For that reason, almost everything included here is in English. But I hope that also scholars will find help in identifying major works in those areas outside of their specialization. This bibliography is intended, first of all, to acquaint students with major works, significant publishers, and prominent scholars in biblical studies. Its second purpose is to assist students in the development of their personal libraries. The inclusion of many titles that are presently out of print should alert the student to the importance of stores and distribution houses that trade in theological used books. The ultimate purpose of the bibliography, however, is to direct students to those works that will be most helpful in interpreting the Bible for preaching and teaching in the church and for personal formation in Christian discipleship. I emphasize interpretation, since all of these works assist in the *exegetical* process. I have not included essentially homiletical or devotional volumes, not because they lack value as such, but because they stand outside the exegetical focus of this bibliography.

I have operated throughout on the basis of a number of assumptions. The first assumption, of course, is that biblical interpretation is foundational for both ministry and personal development in discipleship and is therefore to be pursued with all seriousness. I also assume that although the direct study of the text should be given priority in the interpretive process, this process necessarily involves the employment of secondary sources, in order (1) to aid in the direct study of the text itself (e.g., the use of concordances); (2) to provide knowledge of background (both semantic and historical) that will lead to a "competent" reading, i.e., a reading that makes use of the kind of knowledge the original biblical writer assumed his readers possessed; and (3) to facilitate dialogue with the community of interpreters, recognizing that, in the final analysis, interpretation is a task that God has given to the church as a whole and must be done within in the context of the church's struggle to understand these texts. This final point, however, must not lead to the conclusion that we should consult only those authors who write from the perspective of faith, for all serious and accurate study of the Bible illumines the meaning of the text and is thus helpful for the use of the Bible within the community of faith.

Finally, I assume that there is value in encountering interpreters from various periods and those representing different theological traditions. While affirming the necessity of understanding the Bible according to contemporary issues and the importance of teaching and preaching the Bible to our own age, we should recognize that the parameters of our specific historical existence limit our ability to understand dimensions of the text that were perhaps much clearer to persons who lived in a different age. And while celebrating our participation in our own theological traditions, we should recognize that the meaning of biblical passages is often larger than the construals of individual theological communities, so that our interpretations can be enhanced by insights from those who represent theological commitments other than our own. Hence, I have included authors from a variety of theological traditions, while giving some special consideration at points to evangelical Wesleyan scholarship. And I have incorporated items that represent or discuss interpretive work from different periods, though of necessity giving primary attention to current scholarship, which builds upon the interpretation of the past and carries it forward.

I hope this book will provide assistance to all who work in the area of biblical studies. But I developed this bibliography specifically for the benefit of my own students, and it is to them that I affectionately dedicate it.

My thanks go to Rev. Gary Freymiller, Editor of Evangel Press, who has been gracious and helpful at every point; to my colleague, Dr. Harold Burgess, who made the initial arrangements for publication with Evangel Press; to the members of the Division of Biblical Studies at Asbury Theological Seminary, who were responsible for the first edition of *Biblical Resources for Ministry*, published in 1990; to Asbury Theological Seminary, which provided a grant to underwrite some of the research for this volume; to Mr. Chris Hale and Mr. Timothy Crosby, who gave excellent assistance in bibliographic research; and to Mr. Chris Baker, who compiled the appendix on Bible computer software.

David R. Bauer
Wilmore, Kentucky

THE WHOLE BIBLE

Bibliographic Aids: General

*Allison, Joseph D. *The Bible Study Resource Guide.* Nashville: Nelson, 1982.

*Danker, Frederick W. *Multipurpose Tools for Bible Study.* Rev. ed. Minneapolis: Fortress, 1993.

*Fitzmyer, Joseph A. *An Introductory Bibliography for the Study of Scripture.* Studia Biblica no. 3. 3rd ed. Rome: Biblical Institute, 1990.

Marrow, Stanley B. *Basic Tools of Biblical Exegesis: A Student's Manual.* Rome: Biblical Institute, 1976.

Moo, Douglas. *An Annotated Bibliography on the Bible and the Church.* Deerfield, IL: Trinity Evangelical Divinity School, 1986.

*North, Robert. *Elenchus of Biblica.* 5 vols. Rome: Biblical Institute, 1992—.

Stuart, Douglas. *A Guide to Selecting and Using Bible Commentaries.* Dallas: Word, 1990.

Periodicals

*Bible Review; Bible Today; Biblica; Biblical Interpretation: A Journal of Contemporary Approaches; Biblical Theology Bulletin; *The Catholic Biblical Quarterly; The Expository Times; *Interpretation: A Journal of Bible and Theology; Journal of Biblical Literature; *Tyndale Bulletin.*

History of the Bible

*Ackroyd, Peter R., and Evans, C. F. *Cambridge History of the Bible.* 3 vols. Cambridge: Cambridge University Press, 1988.

Bratton, F. Gladstone. *A History of the Bible.* London: Robert Hale, 1959.

*Bruce, F. F. *The Books and Parchments: How we got our English Bible.* Rev. ed. Old Tappan, NJ: Revell, 1984.

Cunningham, Philip J. *Exploring Scripture: How the Bible Came to Be.* New York: Paulist, 1992.

Ewert, David. *A General Introduction to the Bible: From Ancient Tablets to Modern Translations.* Grand Rapids: Zondervan, 1990.

Koch, Klaus. *The Book of Books: the Growth of the Bible.* Philadelphia: Westminster, 1968.

Norton, David. *A History of the Bible as Literature.* 2 vols. Cambridge: Cambridge University Press, 1993.

Price, Ira M.; Irwin, William A.; and Wikgren, Allen P. *The Ancestry of our English Bible.* 3rd ed. New York: Harper and Row, 1956.

History of the English Bible

American Bible Society. *A Ready-Reference History of the English Bible.* New York: American Bible Society, 1971.

Bailey, Lloyd R., ed. *The Word of God: A Guide to English Versions of the Bible.* Atlanta: John Knox, 1982.

*Bruce, F. F. *History of the Bible in English.* New York: Oxford, 1978.

*Chamberlin, William J. *Catalogue of English Bible Translations: A classified bibliography of versions and editions including books, parts, and Old and New Testament Apocrypha and Apocryphal Books.* New York: Greenwood, 1991.

*Kubo, Sakae, and Specht, Walter. *So Many Versions?* Rev. ed. Grand Rapids: Zondervan, 1983.

*Lewis, Jack P. *The English Bible from KJV to NIV: A History and Evaluation, with Indexes.* 2nd ed. Grand Rapids: Baker, 1991.

History of Interpretation and the Canon (See also under Exegetical Method/Hermeneutics)

Bruce, F. F. *The Canon of Scripture.* Downers Grove, IL: InterVarsity, 1988.

*Coggins, R. J., and Houlden, J. L., eds. *A Dictionary of Biblical Interpretation.* Philadelphia: Trinity Press International, 1990.

*von Campenhausen, Hans. *The Formation of the Christian Bible.* Philadelphia: Fortress, 1972.

Farrar, Frederick W. *History of Interpretation.* New York: Dutton, 1886.

*Frei, Hans. *The Eclipse of Biblical Narrative.* New Haven: Yale, 1974.

Froelich, Karlfried. *Biblical Interpretation in the Early Church.* Sources of Early Christian Thought. Philadelphia: Fortress, 1984.

*Grant, Robert M., and Tracy, David. *A Short History of the Interpretation of the Bible.* 2nd. ed. Philadelphia: Fortress, 1984.

*Kugel, James L., and Green, Rowan A. *Early Biblical Interpretation.* Library of Earliest Christianity. Philadelphia: Westminster, 1986.

McDonald, Lee Martin. *The Formation of the Christian Biblical Canon.* Nashville: Abingdon, 1988.

Miller, John W. *The Origins of the Bible: Rethinking Canon History.* New York: Paulist, 1994.

*Morgan, Robert, and Barton, John. *Biblical Interpretation.* Oxford: Oxford University Press, 1988.

Noll, Mark A. *Between Faith and Criticism: Evangelicals, Scholarship, and the Bible in America.* 2nd ed. San Francisco: Harper & Row, 1991.

Sanders, James A. *From Sacred Story to Sacred Text: Canon as Paradigm.* Philadelphia: Fortress, 1986.

Silva, Moisés. *Has the Church Misread the Bible? The History of Interpretation in the Light of Contemporary Issues.* Grand Rapids: Zondervan, 1987.

Simonetti, Maulio. *Biblical Interpretation in the Early Church: An Historical Introduction to Patristic Exegesis.* Ed. Anders Bergquist and Markus Bockmuehl. Edinburgh: T. & T. Clark, 1994.

Smalley, Beryl. *The Study of the Bible in the Middle Ages.* Oxford: Blackwell, 1952.

Stokes, Mack B. *The Bible in the Wesleyan Heritage.* Nashville: Abingdon, 1981.

Biblical History and Geography (See also under Bible Atlases)

*Aharoni, Yohanan. *The Land of the Bible: A Historical Geography.* Philadelphia: Westminster, 1967.

*Baly, Denis. *Basic Biblical Geography.* Philadelphia: Fortress, 1987.

Corswant, Willy, and Urech, Edouard. *A Dictionary of Life in Bible Times.* New York: Oxford University Press, 1960.

Finegan, Jack. *Myth & Mystery: An Introduction to the Pagan Religions of the Biblical World.* Grand Rapids: Baker, 1989.

*Grabbe, Lester L. *Judaism From Cyrus to Hadrian: Sources, History, Synthesis.* 2 vols. Philadelphia: Fortress, 1992.

Gray, John. *A History of Jerusalem.* London: Robert Hall, 1969.

*Harrison, R. K., ed. *Major Cities of the Biblical World.* New York: Nelson, 1985.

Mathews, Victor H. *Manners and Customs in the Bible.* Peabody, MA: Hendrickson, 1988.

*Orni, Efraim, and Efrat, Elisha. *Geography of Israel.* Jerusalem: Israel Universities Press, 1973.

Pfeiffer, C. F. and Vos, H. F. *The Wycliffe Historical Geography of Bible Lands*. Chicago: Moody, 1967.

Shanks, Hershel, ed. *Ancient Israel: A Short History from Abraham to the Roman Destruction of the Temple*. Washington, DC: Biblical Archaeology Society, 1988.

*Smith, George Adam. *The Historical Geography of the Holy Land*. 25th ed. London: Hodder & Stoughton, 1931; reprint, New York: Harper & Row, 1966.

Turner, George Allan. *Historical Geography of the Holy Land*. Grand Rapids: Baker, 1973.

Bible Atlases

*Aharoni, Yohanan, and Avi-Yonah, Michael. *The Macmillan Bible Atlas*. Rev. ed. New York: Macmillan, 1977.

Bahat, Dan. *Carta's Historical Atlas of Jerusalem*. Jerusalem: Carta, 1973.

*Baly, Denis, and Tushingham, A. D. *Atlas of the Biblical World*. Cleveland: World, 1971.

Beitzel, Barry. *The Moody Atlas of Bible Lands*. Chicago: Moody, 1986.

Bimson, J. J.; Kane, J. P.; Paterson, J. H.; et al., eds. *New Bible Atlas*. Downers Grove, IL: InterVarsity, 1985.

Frank, Harry Thomas, ed. *Hammond's Atlas of the Bible Lands: An Illustrated Atlas of the Bible*. New ed. Maplewood, NJ: Hammond, 1984.

Hooper, Jerry L., ed. *The Holman Bible Atlas*. Philadelphia: Holman, 1978.

*Kraeling, Emil G. H. *Rand McNally Bible Atlas*. Edited by Carl H. Kraeling. New York: Rand McNally, n.d.

*May, Herbert G. *Oxford Bible Atlas.* 2nd ed. London: Oxford, 1974.

*Pritchard, James B. *Harper's Atlas of the Bible.* San Francisco: Harper, 1987.

Rasmussen, Carl. *The Zondervan NIV Atlas of the Bible.* Grand Rapids: Zondervan, 1989.

*Wright, G. Ernest, and Filson, Floyd V., eds. *The Westminster Historical Atlas to the Bible.* Rev. ed. Philadelphia: Westminster, 1956.

Biblical Archaeology (See also under Exegetical Method/Hermeneutics of the Old Testament)

Albright, William Foxwell. *The Archaeology of Palestine.* Harmondsworth: Penguin, 1949.

*Blaiklock, E. M., and Harrison, R. K., eds. *The New Dictionary of Biblical Archaeology.* Grand Rapids: Zondervan, 1983.

Campbell, Edward F., and Freedman, David Noel. *The Biblical Archaeologist Reader.* 3 vols. New York: Doubleday, 1961-1970.

———. *Biblical Archaeologist Reader, IV.* Sheffield: Almond, 1983.

*Charlesworth, James H., and Weaver, Walter P., eds. *What Has Archaeology to do With Faith?* Faith and Scholarship Colloquies. Valley Forge, PA: Trinity Press International, 1992.

*Finegan, Jack. *Introduction to Israel: An Archaeological Guide to the Holy Land.* Grand Rapids: Eerdmans, 1981.

———. *Light From the Ancient Past.* Princeton, NJ: Princeton University Press, 1959.

*Fritz, Volkmar. *An Introduction to Biblical Archaeology.* Journal for the Study of the Old Testament Supplement Series, no. 172. Sheffield: JSOT, 1994.

*Hoppe, Leslie J. *What are They Saying about Biblical Archaeology?* New York: Paulist, 1989.

Kenyon, Kathleen M. *Archeology in the Holy Land.* 4th ed. New York: Norton, 1979.

*Lance, H. Darrell. *The Old Testament and the Archaeologist.* Guides to Biblical Scholarship. Philadelphia: Fortress, 1981.

*Mazar, Amihac. *Archaeology of the Land of the Bible: 10,000-586 B.C.E.* Anchor Bible Reference Library. Garden City, NJ: Doubleday, 1990.

*Morrey, P. R. S. *A Century of Biblical Archaeology.* Louisville: Westminster/John Knox, 1991.

Rousseau, John J. and Arav, Rami (with Carol Meyers). *Jesus and His World: An Archaeological and Cultural Dictionary.* Philadelphia: Fortress, 1994.

Schoville, Keith. *Biblical Archaeology in Focus.* Grand Rapids: Baker, 1978.

*Stern, Ephraim. *The New Encyclopedia of Archaeological Excavations in the Holy Land.* 4 vols. New York: Simon & Schuster, 1993.

Thomas, D. Winton, ed. *Archeology and Old Testament Study.* Oxford: Clarendon, 1967.

*Thompson, J. A. *Biblical Archaeology.* Grand Rapids: Eerdmans, 1981.

Wheeler, Mortimer. *Archaeology from the Earth.* Baltimore: Penguin, 1954.

Wright, G. Ernest. *Biblical Archaeology.* Philadelphia: Westminster, 1957.

(See also these journals: *Archaeology in the Biblical World; The Biblical Archaeological Review; The Biblical Archaeologist*)

Concordances to the English Bible

Cruden, Alexander. *A Complete Concordance to the Holy Scriptures of the Old and New Testament.* London: [s.n. 1737?]; reprint, Grand Rapids: Zondervan, 1968.

*Ellison, John W. *Nelson's Complete Concordance of the Revised Standard Version of the Bible.* New York, 1957.

*Goodrich, Edward W., and Kohlenberger III, John R. *The NIV Exhaustive Concordance.* Grand Rapids: Zondervan, 1981.

*Kohlenberger III, John R. *The NRSV Concordance, Unabridged.* Grand Rapids: Zondervan, 1991.

*Strong, James. *The Exhaustive Concordance of the Bible.* New York: Abingdon, 1890; reprint, Nashville: Nelson, 1984.

*Thomas, Robert L., ed. *NAS Exhaustive Concordance.* Nashville: Broadman & Holman, 1981.

Whitaker, Richard E. *RSV Analytical Concordance.* Grand Rapids: Eerdmans, 1988.

*Young, Robert. *Analytical Concordance to the Bible.* Rev. ed. Nashville: Nelson, 1982.

Topical Concordances

Day, A. Colin. *Roget's Thesaurus of the Bible.* San Francisco: Harper, 1992.

*Hitchcock, Roswell D. *Baker's Topical Bible.* Grand Rapids: Baker, 1975.

Joy, Charles R., Jr. *Harper's Topical Concordance.* Rev. ed. New York: Harper & Row, 1962.

*Kohlenberger III, John R. *Zondervan NIV Nave's Topical Bible.* Grand Rapids: Zondervan, 1992.

Bible Dictionaries

*Achtemeier, Paul J. ed. *Harper's Bible Dictionary.* San Francisco: Harper & Row, 1985.

*Bromiley, Geoffrey W., ed. *International Standard Bible Encyclopedia.* Rev. ed. 4 vols. Grand Rapids: Eerdmans, 1979-1988.

*Buttrick George A., ed. *The Interpreter's Dictionary of the Bible.* 4 vols.+Supplementary Volume. Nashville: Abingdon, 1962, 1976.

Douglas, J. D., et al., eds. *The New Bible Dictionary.* Downers Grove, IL: InterVarsity, 1984.

*Freedman, David Noel, ed. *The Anchor Bible Dictionary.* 6 vols. New York: Doubleday, 1992.

Hastings, James, ed. *Dictionary of the Bible.* 5 vols. Edinburgh: T. & T. Clark, 1898.

Myers, Allen C. *The Eerdmans Bible Dictionary.* Rev. ed. Grand Rapids: Eerdmans, 1987.

Tenney, Merrill C. *The Zondervan Pictorial Encyclopedia of the Bible.* 5 vols. Grand Rapids: Zondervan, 1975.

Exegetical Method/Hermeneutics

Alter, Robert. *The World of Biblical Literature.* San Francisco: Harper, 1993.

Barr, James. *The Semantics of Biblical Language.* London: SCM, 1961.

*Carson, D. A. *Exegetical Fallacies.* Grand Rapids: Baker, 1984.

Cotterell, Peter, and Turner, Max. *Linguistics & Biblical Interpretation.* Downers Grove, IL: InterVarsity, 1989.

*Fee, Gordon D., and Stuart, Douglas. *How to Read the Bible for All Its Worth.* Grand Rapids: Zondervan, 1982.

Ferguson, Duncan S. *Biblical Hermeneutics: An Introduction.* Atlanta: John Knox, 1986.

*Goldingay, John. *Models for the Interpretation of Scripture.* Grand Rapids: Eerdmans, 1994.

*Hayes, John H., and Holladay, Carl R. *Biblical Exegesis: A Beginner's Handbook.* Rev. ed. Atlanta: John Knox, 1987.

*Kaiser, Otto, and Kümmel, Werner Georg. *Exegetical Method: A Student's Handbook.* New York: Seabury, 1967.

Kaiser, Walter C., Jr. *Toward an Exegetical Theology: Biblical Exegesis for Preaching and Teaching.* Grand Rapids: Baker, 1981.

Klein, William W.; Blomberg, Craig L.; and Hubbard, Robert L. *Introduction to Biblical Interpretation.* Dallas: Word, 1993.

Krentz, Edgar. *The Historical-Critical Method.* Guides to Biblical Scholarship. Philadelphia: Fortress, 1975.

Kuist, Howard T. *These Words Upon Thy Heart: Scripture and the Christian Response.* Richmond: John Knox, 1947.

Longman III, Tremper. *Literary Approaches to Biblical Interpretation.* Foundations of Contemporary Interpretation, vol. 3. Grand Rapids: Zondervan, 1987.

McCown, Wayne, and Massey, James, eds. *God's Word for Today: An Inquiry into Hermeneutics from a Biblical Theological Perspective.* Wesleyan Theological Perspectives, no. 2. Anderson, IN: Warner, 1982.

McKim, Donald K., ed. *A Guide to Contemporary Hermeneutics: Major Trends in Biblical Interpretation.* Grand Rapids: Eerdmans, 1986.

McKnight, Edgar V. *The Bible and the Reader: An Introduction to Literary Criticism.* Philadelphia: Fortress, 1985.

Mickelsen, A. Berkeley, and Mickelsen, Alvera M. *Understanding Scripture: How to Read and Study the Bible.* Peabody, MA: Hendrickson, 1992.

Morgan, Robert, and Barton, John. *Biblical Interpretation.* Oxford
Bible Series. Oxford: Oxford University Press, 1988.

Mulholland, M. Robert, Jr. *Shaped by the Word: The Power of Scripture
in Spiritual Formation.* Nashville: Upper Room, 1985.

Osborne, Grant R. *The Hermeneutical Spiral.* Downers Grove, IL:
InterVarsity, 1992.

Ramm, Bernard L. *Protestant Biblical Interpretation: A Textbook of
Hermeneutics for Conservative Protestants.* 3rd. ed. Grand Rapids:
Baker, 1970.

Ricoeur, Paul. *Essays on Biblical Interpretation.* Philadelphia: Fortress,
1980.

Silva, Moisés. *God, Language, and Scripture: Reading the Bible in Light
of General Linguistics.* Grand Rapids: Zondervan, 1990.

*———. *Biblical Words and their Meaning: An Introduction to Lexical
Semantics.* Grand Rapids: Zondervan, 1983.

Soulen, Richard N. *Handbook of Biblical Criticism.* 2nd ed. Atlanta:
John Knox, 1981.

Terry, Milton S. *Biblical Hermeneutics.* New York: Eaton and Mains,
1911; reprint, Grand Rapids: Zondervan, 1969.

*Thiselton, Anthony C. *New Horizons in Hermeneutics: The Theory and
Practice of Transforming Biblical Reading.* Grand Rapids:
Zondervan, 1992.

Thompson, David L. *Bible Study that Works.* Rev. ed. Nappanee, IN:
Evangel, 1994.

*Traina, Robert A. *Methodical Bible Study: A New Approach to
Hermeneutics.* New York: Ganis & Harris, 1952; reprint, Grand
Rapids: Zondervan, 1985.

Wink, Walter. *Transforming Bible Study: Completely Revised and
Expanded.* Nashville: Abingdon, 1990.

(Account should be taken here of the series, "Guide to Biblical
Scholarship," published by Fortress. See under
Method/Hermeneutics in the Old Testament, and
Method/Hermeneutics in the New Testament for specific vol-
umes.)

Biblical Theology

Achtemeier, Paul J., and Elizabeth R. *The Old Testament Roots of our
Faith.* Rev. ed. Peabody, MA: Hendrickson, 1995.

Bauer, Johannes Baptiste, ed. *Encyclopedia of Biblical Theology: The
Complete Sacramentum Verbi.* Rev. ed. New York: Crossroad,
1981.

*Bright, John. *The Kingdom of God.* Nashville: Abingdon, 1953.

Burrows, Millar. *An Outline of Biblical Theology.* Philadelphia:
Westminster, 1946.

*Childs, Brevard S. *Biblical Theology in Crisis.* Philadelphia: Fortress,
1970.

*———. *Biblical Theology of the Old and New Testaments: Theological
Reflection on the Christian Bible.* Minneapolis: Fortress, 1993.

*Cullmann, Oscar. *Salvation in History.* New York: Harper & Row,
1967.

Gerhardsson, Birger. *The Ethos of the Bible.* Philadelphia: Fortress,
1981.

*Leon-Dufour, Xavier. *Dictionary of Biblical Theology.* 2nd ed. New
York: Seabury, 1973.

*Reumann, John H. P. *The Promise and Practice of Biblical Theology.*
Philadelphia: Fortress, 1991.

Smart, James D. *The Past, Present, and Future of Biblical Theology.*
Philadelphia: Westminster, 1979.

Stuhlmacher, Peter. *How To Do Biblical Theology.* Allison Park, PA: Pickwick, 1995.

Turner, George Allen. *The Vision which Transforms: Is Christian Perfection Scriptural?* Kansas City, MS: Beacon Hill, 1964.

Vos, Geerhardus. *Biblical Theology: Old and New Testaments.* Grand Rapids: Eerdmans, 1948.

Biblical Ethics

*Birch, Bruce C., and Rasmussen, Larry L. *Bible and Ethics in the Christian Life.* Minneapolis: Augsburg, 1976.

Everding, H. Edward, Jr., and Wilbanks, Dana W. *Decision-making and the Bible.* Valley Forge, PA: Judson, 1975.

*McDonald, J. I. H. *Biblical Interpretation and Christian Ethics.* Cambridge: Cambridge University Press, 1993.

Ogletree, Thomas W. *The Use of the Bible in Christian Ethics.* Philadelphia: Westminster, 1983.

Sleeper, C. Freeman. *The Bible and the Moral Life.* Louisville: Westminster/John Knox, 1992.

*Spohn, William C. *What Are They Saying about Scripture and Ethics?* New York: Paulist, 1984.

Bible Commentaries

One-volume commentaries include:

*Brown, Raymond E.; Fitzmyer, Joseph A.; and Murphy, Roland E., eds. *The New Jerome Bible Commentary.* Englewood Cliffs, NJ: Prenctice-Hall, 1990.

*Carpenter, Eugene, and McCown, Wayne, eds. *Asbury Bible Commentary.* Grand Rapids: Zondervan, 1992.

Carson, D.A.; France R. T.; Wenham, Gordon; and Motyer, James A., eds. *New Bible Commentary: 21st Century Edition.* Downers Grove, IL: InterVarsity, 1994.

Guthrie, Donald, and Motyer, J. A., ed. *The New Bible Commentary.* 3rd ed. London: InterVarsity, 1970.

Laymon, Charles M., ed. *The Interpreter's One-Volume Commentary on the Bible.* Nashville: Abingdon, 1971.

*Mays, James Luther, ed. *Harper's Bible Commentary.* San Francisco: Harper & Row, 1988.

Peake, Arthur S., ed. *A Commentary on the Bible.* New York: T. Nelson, 1920.

Multi-volume commentaries include:

Buttrick, George Arthur, ed. *The Interpreter's Bible.* 12 vols. Nashville: Abingdon, 1952.

*Calvin, John. *Calvin's Commentaries.* 22 vols. Grand Rapids: Baker, 1979. (Originally published, in Latin and French, ca. 1550-1555.)

Carter, Charles W., ed. *The Wesleyan Bible Commentary.* 7 vols. Grand Rapids: Eerdmans, 1964-69.

Clarke, Adam. *Clarke's Commentary.* 8 vols. London: Butterworth, 1810-1825; reprint (6 vols. in 3), Nashville: Abingdon, 1977.

Gaebelein, Frank E., and Douglas, J. D., ed. *The Expositor's Bible Commentary.* Grand Rapids: Zondervan, 1979.

Keck, Leander, et al., eds. *The New Interpreter's Bible.* 12 vols. Nashville: Abingdon, 1994. (Two volumes are presently available.)

Lange, John Peter, ed. *A Commentary on the Holy Scripture.* Edited by Philip Schaff. 24 vols. New York: Scribner's, 1865-79.

*Nicoll, W. Robertson, ed. *The Expositor's Bible.* 25 vols. New York: Armstrong, 1903.

Purkiser, W. T., and Earle, Ralph, eds. *Beacon Bible Commentary*. 10 vols. Kansas City, MO: Beacon Hill, 1969.

Multi-volume commentary series whose individual volumes are frequently listed below under specific biblical books include:

The Anchor Bible: A New Translation with Introduction and Commentary, ed. William Foxwell Albright, and David Noel Freedman (Doubleday); *Cambridge Bible Commentary on the New English Bible*, ed. P. R. Ackroyd; A. R. C. Leaney; and J. W. Packer (Cambridge); *Hermeneia: A Critical and Historical Commentary on the Bible*, ed. Frank Moore Cross, and Helmut Koester (Fortress); *The International Critical Commentary*, ed. S. R. Driver, Alfred Plummer, and C. A. Briggs (original series), ed. J. A. Emerton, and C. E. B. Cranfield (new series)(T. & T. Clark); *Interpretation: A Bible Commentary for Teaching and Preaching*, ed. James Luther Mays (John Knox); *New Century Bible*, ed. Ronald E. Clements, and Matthew Black (Eerdmans); *Word Biblical Commentaries*, ed. David A. Hubbard, and Glenn W. Barker (Word). With this kind of multi-volume commentaries, it is generally advisable to select individual volumes rather than purchase the whole set; individual volumes tend to vary in terms of quality and usefulness.

See also extended commentary by the church fathers (e.g., St. Augustine and St. John Chrysostom) in Schaff, Philip, ed. *The Nicene and Post-Nicene Fathers*. 14 vols. A Select Library of the Christian Church. Peabody, MA: Hendrickson, 1994.

THE OLD TESTAMENT

Bibliographic Aids (See also under History of Interpretation, and Introductions.)

Auld, A. Graeme. *Society for Old Testament Study Booklist, 1990.* Sheffield: JSOT, 1990.

*Barker, Kenneth L.; Waltke, Bruce K.; and Zuck, Roy B. *Bibliography for Old Testament Exegesis and Exposition.* 4th ed. Dallas: Dallas Theological Seminary, 1979.

*Childs, Brevard S. *Old Testament Books for Pastor and Teacher.* Philadelphia: Westminster, 1977.

Zannoni, Arthur E. *The Old Testament: A Bibliography.* Collegeville, MN: Michael Glazier, 1992.

Periodicals

Journal for the Study of the Old Testament; Old Testament Abstracts; Vetus Testamentum.

History of Interpretation and the Canon (See also under Old Testament Introductions)

*Beckwith, Roger T. *The Old Testament Canon of the New Testament Church and its Background in Early Judaism.* Grand Rapids: Eerdmans, 1985.

Clements, Ronald E. *One Hundred Years of Old Testament Interpretation.* Philadelphia: Westminster, 1976.

*Fishbane, Michael. *Biblical Interpretation in Ancient Israel.* Oxford: Clarendon, 1985.

*Knight, Douglas A., and Tucker, Gene M., eds. *The Hebrew Bible and its Modern Interpreters.* Chico, CA: Scholars, 1985.

*Kraeling, Emil G. H. *The Old Testament Since the Reformation.* New York: Harper, 1955.

Levenson, Jon D. *The Hebrew Bible, the Old Testament, and Historical Criticism: Jews and Christians in Biblical Studies.* Philadelphia: Westminster, 1993.

Rogerson, John William. *Old Testament Criticism in the Nineteenth Century.* Philadelphia: Fortress, 1985.

Rowley, H. H. *Growth of the Old Testament.* London: Hutchinson's University, 1964.

Sanders, James A. *Torah and Canon.* Philadelphia: Fortress, 1972.

History and Geography

Ackroyd, Peter R. *Exile and Restoration: A Study of Hebrew Thought of the Sixth Century B.C.* Old Testament Library. Philadelphia: Westminster, 1975.

*Ahlstrom, Gösta W. *The History of Ancient Palestine.* Minneapolis: Fortress, 1993.

*Albertz, Rainer. *A History of Israelite Religion in the Old Testament Period.* 2 vols. Old Testament Library. Louisville: Westminster/John Knox, 1994.

*Bright, John. *A History of Israel.* 3rd ed. Philadelphia: Westminster, 1981.

Clements, Ronald E. *The World of Ancient Israel: Sociological, Anthropological, and Political Perspectives.* Cambridge: Cambridge University Press, 1991.

de Vaux, Roland. *Ancient Israel: Its Life and Institutions.* 2 vols. New York: McGraw-Hill, 1965.

*Hayes, John H., and Miller, J. Maxwell, eds. *Israelite and Judaean History.* Old Testament Library. Philadelphia: Westminster, 1977.

Kaufmann, Yehezkel. *The Religion of Israel: From its Beginnings to the Babylonian Exile.* New York: Schocken, 1960.

Mathews, Victor H., and Benjamin, Don C. *Social World of Ancient Israel, 1250-587 BCE.* Peabody, MA: Hendrickson, 1993.

Noth, Martin. *The History of Israel.* 2nd ed. New York: Harper & Row, 1960.

*Schmidt, Werner H. *The Faith of the Old Testament: A History.* Philadelphia: Westminster, 1983.

Wellhausen, Julius. *Prologomena to the History of Israel: with a reprint of the article "Israel" from the Encyclopaedia Brittanica.* Edinburgh: A. & C. Black, 1885; reprint, Gloucester, MA: Peter Smith, 1973.

Wiseman, Donald J. *Peoples of the Old Testament.* Oxford: Oxford University Press, 1973.

Wood, Leon. *A Survey of Israel's History.* Revised by D. McBride. Grand Rapids: Zondervan, 1986.

Ancient Near Eastern Literature and Art

*Beyerlin, Walter, ed. *Near Eastern Religious Texts Relating to the Old Testament.* Old Testament Library. Philadelphia: Westminster, 1978.

*Pritchard, James B., ed. *Ancient Near Eastern Texts Relating to the Old Testament.* 3rd ed. with supplement. Princeton: Princeton University Press, 1969.

———, ed. *The Ancient Near East: An Anthology of Texts and Pictures.* 2 vols. Princeton: Princeton University Press, 1958, 1976.

———. *The Ancient Near East in Pictures Related to the Old Testament.* Princeton: Princeton University Press, 1954.

Hebrew Grammars

Davidson, A. B. *Hebrew Syntax*. Edinburgh: T. & T. Clark, 1894.

*Driver, S. R. *A Treatise on the Use of the Tenses in Hebrew*. 3rd ed. Oxford: Clarendon, 1892.

Jouon, S. J., and Muraoka, T. *A Grammar of Biblical Hebrew*. 2 vols. Subsidia Biblica, vols. 14/I-II. Rome: Biblical Institute, 1991.

*Kautzsch, E, ed. *Gesenius' Hebrew Grammar*. 2nd ed. Revised by A. E. Cowley. Oxford: Clarendon, 1909.

Lambdin, T. O. *Introduction to Biblical Hebrew*. New York: Scribner's, 1971.

*LaSor, W. S. *Handbook of Biblical Hebrew*. Grand Rapids: Eerdmans, 1988.

Waldman, Nahum M. *The Recent Study of Hebrew: A Survey of the Literature with Selected Bibliography*. Winona Lake, IN: Eisenbrauns, 1989.

*Waltke, Bruce K., and O'Connor, M. *An Introduction to Biblical Hebrew Syntax*. Winona Lake, IN: Eisenbrauns, 1990.

Williams, Ronald J. *Hebrew Syntax: An Outline*. Toronto: University of Toronto Press, 1976.

Hebrew Lexicons

Armstrong, Terry A.; Busby, Douglas L.; and Carr, Cyril F. *A Reader's Hebrew-English Lexicon of the Old Testament*. Grand Rapids: Zondervan, 1989.

*Brown, Francis; Driver, S. R.; and Briggs, Charles A. *A Hebrew and English Lexicon of the Old Testament*. Oxford: Oxford University Press, 1907; reprint, Peabody, MA: Hendrickson, 1979 (indexed to Strong's).

Clines, David J. A., ed. *The Dictionary of Classical Hebrew.* 8 vols.
Sheffield: Sheffield Academic Press, 1993. (Volume 1 is presently
available.)

Davidson, Benjamin. *The Analytical Hebrew and Chaldee Lexicon.*
Grand Rapids: Zondervan, 1971.

Fohrer, Georg, ed. *Hebrew and Aramaic Dictionary of the Old Testament.*
Berlin: DeGruyter, 1973.

*Holladay, William L. *A Concise Hebrew and Aramaic Lexicon of the Old
Testament.* Grand Rapids: Eerdmans, 1971.

*Koehler, L. and Baumgartner, W. *The Hebrew and Aramaic Lexicon of
the Old Testament.* Revised by Walter Baumgartner and Johann
Jakob Stamm. 4 vols. Leiden: Brill, 1994.
(Volume 1 is presently available.)

Theological Dictionaries (Wordbooks)

*Botterweck, G. Johannes, and Ringgren, Helmer, eds. *Theological
Dictionary of the Old Testament.* Grand Rapids: Eerdmans, 1974-
95. (vols. 1-7 are presently available)

*Harris, R. L.; Archer, G. L.; and Waltke, B. K. eds. *Theological
Wordbook of the Old Testament.* 2 vols. Chicago: Moody, 1980.

(See also the discussions of Old Testament terms found in *Theological
Dictionary of the New Testament,* and the discussions of Old
Testament passages and concepts found in Barth's *Church
Dogmatics.*)

Concordances to the Hebrew Bible

*Even-Shoshan, Abraham. *A New Concordance of the Old Testament.*
Grand Rapids: Baker, 1984.

Lisowsky, Gerhard. *Konkordanz zum Hebraischen Alten Testament.* 2nd
ed. Stuttgart: Wurttembergische Bibelanstalt, 1958.

Mandelkern, Solomon. *Veteris Testamenti Concordantiae: Hebraica atqua Chaldaicae.* Tel Aviv: Sumptibus Schocken Hierosolymis, 1971.

*Wigram, George V. *The Englishman's Hebrew and Chaldee Concordance of the Old Testament: Numerically Coded to Strong's Exhaustive Concordance.* 5th ed. Grand Rapids: Zondervan, 1980.

Textual Criticism

*McCarter, P. Kyle. *Textual Criticism: Recovering the Text of the Hebrew Bible.* Guides to Biblical Scholarship. Philadelphia: Fortress, 1986.

*Tov, Emanuel. *Textual Criticism of the Hebrew Bible.* Philadelphia: Fortress, 1993.

Wonneberger, Reinhard. *Understanding BHS: A Manual for Users of Biblica Hebraica Stuttgartensia.* 2nd ed. Subsidia Biblical, vol. 8. Rome: Biblical Institute, 1990.

*Würthwein, E. *The Text of the Old Testament.* Rev. ed. Grand Rapids: Eerdmans, 1994.

Exegetical Method/Hermeneutics

*Achtemeier, Elizabeth. *Preaching from the Old Testament.* Louisville: Westminster/John Knox, 1989.

*Alter, Robert. *The Art of Biblical Narrative.* San Francisco: Harper, 1983.

*———. *The Art of Biblical Poetry.* San Francisco: Harper, 1987.

Armerding, Carl. E. *The Old Testament and Criticism.* Grand Rapids: Eerdmans, 1983.

Barton, John. *Reading the Old Testament: Method in Biblical Study.* Philadelphia: Westminster, 1984

Exum, J. Cheryl, and Clines, David J. A., eds. *The New Literary Criticism and the Hebrew Bible.* Sheffield: JSOT, 1993.

*Goldingay, John. *Approaches to Old Testament Interpretation.* Rev. ed. Downers Grove, IL: InterVarsity, 1990.

*———. *Models for Interpretation of Scripture.* Grand Rapids: Eerdmans, 1995.

Gowan, Donald E. *Reclaiming the Old Testament for the Christian Pulpit.* Atlanta: John Knox, 1980.

Gunn, David M., and Fewell, Danna Nolan. *Narrative in the Hebrew Bible.* Oxford Bible Series. Oxford: Oxford University Press, 1993.

Gunneweg, A. H. S. *Understanding the Old Testament.* Philadelphia: Westminster, 1978.

Hanson, Paul D. *Old Testament Apocalyptic.* Interpreting Biblical Texts. Nashville: Abingdon, 1987.

Hayes, John, ed. *Old Testament Form Criticism.* San Antonio: Trinity University Press, 1974.

Koch, Klaus. *The Growth of the Biblical Tradition: The Form-Critical Method.* New York: Scribner's, 1969.

Kugel, James L. *The Idea of Biblical Poetry: Parallelism and its History.* New Haven, CT: Yale University Press, 1981.

McCurley, Foster R. *Proclaiming the Promise: Christian Preaching from the Old Testament.* Philadelphia: Fortress, 1974.

von Rad, Gerhard. *Biblical Interpretations in Preaching.* Nashville: Abingdon, 1977.

*Stuart, Douglas. *Old Testament Exegesis: A Primer for Students and Pastors.* 2nd ed. Philadelphia: Westminster, 1984.

Westermann, Claus, ed. *Essays on Old Testament Hermeneutics.* Atlanta: John Knox, 1963.

The following volumes in "Guides to Biblical Scholarship" are relevant:

Habel, Norman C. *Literary Criticism of the Old Testament.* Philadelphia: Fortress, 1971.

Miller, J. Maxwell. *The Old Testament and the Historian.* Philadelphia: Fortress, 1976.

Niditch, Susan. *Folklore and the Hebrew Bible.* Minneapolis: Fortress, 1983.

*Petersen, David L., and Richards, Kent Harold. *Interpreting Hebrew Poetry.* Minneapolis: Fortress, 1992.

Rast, Walter E. *Tradition History and the Old Testament.* Philadelphia: Fortress, 1972.

*Sanders, James A. *Canon and Community: A Guide to Canonical Criticism.* Philadelphia: Fortress, 1984.

*Trible, Phyllis. *Rhetorical Criticism: Context, Method, and the Book of Jonah.* Minneapolis: Fortress, 1994.

*Tucker, Gene M. *Form Criticism of the Old Testament.* Philadelphia: Fortress, 1971.

*Wilson, Robert R. *Sociological Approaches to the Old Testament.* Philadelphia: Fortress, 1984.

Old Testament Surveys

*Anderson, Bernhard W. *Understanding the Old Testament.* 3rd ed. Englewood Cliffs, NJ: Prentic-Hall, 1975.

*Craigie, Peter C. *The Old Testament: Its Background, Growth, & Content.* Nashville: Abingdon, 1986.

Hill, Andrew E., and Walton, John H. *A Survey of the Old Testament.* Grand Rapids: Zondervan, 1991.

LaSor, W. S., et al. *Old Testament Survey.* Grand Rapids: Eerdmans, 1978.

Marshall, Celia Brewer. *A Guide through the Old Testament.* Louisville: Westminster/John Knox, 1989.

*Schultz, Samuel, *The Old Testament Speaks.* 4th ed. New York: Harper, 1990.

Old Testament Introductions

*Childs, Brevard S. *Introduction to the Old Testament as Scripture.* Philadelphia: Fortress, 1979.

Crenshaw, James L. *Old Testament Story and Faith: A Literary & Theological Introduction.* Peabody, MA: Hendrickson, 1992.

Eissfeldt, Otto. *The Old Testament: An Introduction.* New York: Harper & Row, 1965.

Gottwald, Norman K. *The Hebrew Bible: A Socio-Literary Introduction.* Philadelphia: Fortress, 1985.

*Harrison, R. K. *Introduction to the Old Testament.* Grand Rapids: Eerdmans, 1969.

*Hayes, John H. *An Introduction to Old Testament Study.* Nashville: Abingdon, 1979.

Kaiser, Otto. *Introduction to the Old Testament.* Oxford: Blackwell, 1975.

*Orr, James. *The Problem of the Old Testament Considered with reference to Recent Criticism.* New York: Scribner's, 1906.

Rendtorff, Rolf. *The Old Testament: An Introduction.* Philadelphia: Fortress, 1985.

Sandmel, Samuel. *The Hebrew Scriptures: An Introduction to Their Literature and Religious Ideas.* Oxford: Oxford University Press, 1978.

*Schmidt, Werner H. *Old Testament Introduction.* New York: Crossroad, 1990.

Sellin, Ernst, and Fohrer, Georg. *Introduction to the Old Testament.* Rev. ed. Nashville: Abingdon, 1968.

*Smith, W. Robertson. *The Old Testament in the Jewish Church.* New York: Appleton, 1881.

Soggin, J. A. *Introduction to the Old Testament.* Old Testament Library. Philadelphia: Westminster, 1976.

Young, Edward J. *An Introduction to the Old Testament.* Grand Rapids: Eerdmans, 1949.

Old Testament Theology

Anderson, Bernhard W. *From Creation to New Creation: Old Testament Perspectives.* Overtures to Biblical Theology. Minneapolis: Fortress, 1994.

Barth, Christoph. *God With Us: A Theological Introduction to the Old Testament.* Grand Rapids: Eerdmans, 1991.

*Bright, John. *The Authority of the Old Testament.* Nashville: Abingdon, 1967; reprint, Grand Rapids: Baker, 1975.

Brueggemann, Walter. *Old Testament Theology: Essays on Structure, Theme, and Text.* Edited by Patrick D. Miller, Jr. Minneapolis: Fortress, 1991.

*Childs, Brevard S. *Old Testament Theology in a Canonical Context.* Philadelphia: Fortress, 1985.

Davidson, A. B. *The Theology of the Old Testament.* The International Theological Library. Edinburgh: T. & T. Clark, 1904.

*Eichrodt, Walther. *Theology of the Old Testament.* 2 vols. Old Testament Library. Philadelphia: Westminster, 1967.

Goldingay, John. *Theological Diversity and the Authority of the Old Testament.* Grand Rapids: Eerdmans, 1987.

Hasel, Gerhard. *Old Testament Theology: Basic Issues in the Current Debate.* 4th ed. Grand Rapids: Eerdmans, 1991.

Hayes, John H., and Prussner, Frederick. *Old Testament Theology: Its History and Development.* Atlanta: John Knox, 1985.

Kaiser, Walter C., Jr. *Toward an Old Testament Theology.* Grand Rapids: Zondervan, 1978.

Ollenburger, Ben C.; Martens, Elmer A.; and Hasel, Gerhard F., eds. *The Flowering of Old Testament Theology.* Sources for Biblical and Theological Study, no. 1. Winona Lake, IN: Eisenbrauns, 1992.

*von Rad, Gerhard. *Old Testament Theology.* 2 vols. New York: Harper & Row, 1962.

*Rendtorff, Rolf. *Canon and Theology: Overtures to an Old Testament Theology.* Overtures to Biblical Theology. Minneapolis: Fortress, 1993.

Reventlow, Henning Graf. *Problems of Old Testament Theology in the Twentieth Century.* Philadelphia: Fortress, 1985.

Snaith, Norman H. *The Distinctive Ideas of the Old Testament.* New York: Schocken, 1964.

Vriezen, Theodorus Christiaan. *An Outline of Old Testament Theology.* Oxford: Blackwell, 1962.

*Westermann, Claus. *Elements of Old Testament Theology.* Atlanta: John Knox, 1982.

Wright, G. Ernest. *God who Acts: Biblical Theology as Recital.* Studies in Biblical Theology, no. 8. London: SCM, 1952.

Zimmerli, Walther. *Old Testament Theology in Outline.* Atlanta: John Knox, 1978.

Old Testament Ethics

*Birch, Bruce C. *Let Justice Roll Down: The Old Testament, Ethics, and the Christian Life.* Louisville: Westminster/John Knox, 1991.

*Birch, Bruce C. *What Does the Lord Require?: The Old Testament Call to Social Witness.* Louisville: Westminster/John Knox, 1985.

*Janzen, Waldemar. *Old Testament Ethics: A Paradigmatic Approach.* Louisville: Westminster/John Knox, 1994.

Kaiser, Walter C., Jr. *Toward Old Testament Ethics.* Grand Rapids: Zondervan, 1983.

Wright, Christopher J. H. *An Eye for an Eye: The Place of Old Testament Ethics Today.* Downers Grove, IL: InterVarsity, 1983.

Old Testament Commentaries

*Keil, Carl Friedrich, and Delitzsch, Franz. *Commentary on the Old Testament.* 10 vols. Grand Rapids: Eerdmans, 1976. Reprint of various editions and various printings, 1880—.

*Wesley, John. *Wesley's Notes on the Bible.* Edited by Lawrence Schoenhals. Grand Rapids: Francis Asbury, 1987.

Multi-volume commentary series whose individual volumes are frequently listed below under specific biblical books include:

New International Commentary on the Old Testament, ed. R. K. Harrison (Eerdmans); *International Theological Commentary,* ed. George A. F. Knight, and Fredrick Carlson Holmgren (Eerdmans); *Old Testament Library,* ed. Peter Ackroyd, James Barr, John Bright, and G. Ernest Wright (Westminster); *Proclamation Commentaries: The Old Testament Witnesses for Preaching,* ed. Foster R. McCurley (Fortress); *Daily Study Bible: Old Testament,* ed. John C. L. Gibson (Westminster). With this kind of multi-volume commentaries, it is generally advisable to select individual volumes rather than purchase the whole set; individual volumes tend to vary in terms of quality and usefulness.

The Pentateuch: General Works

*Bailey, Lloyd R. *The Pentateuch.* Interpreting Biblical Texts Nashville: Abingdon, 1981.

*Blenkinsopp, Joseph. *The Pentateuch: An Introduction to the First Five Books of the Bible.* Anchor Bible Reference Library. New York: Doubleday, 1992.

*Brueggemann, Walter, and Wolff, Hans Walter. *The Vitality of Old Testament Traditions.* Atlanta: John Knox, 1978.

Buber, Martin. *Moses: The Revelation and the Covenant.* New York: Harper, 1958.

Clines, David J. A. *The Theme of the Pentateuch.* Sheffield: JSOT, 1978.

Coats, George W. *Moses: Heroic Man, Man of God.* Journal for the Study of the Old Testament Supplement Series, no. 57. Sheffield: JSOT, 1988.

Hamilton, Victor P. *Handbook on the Pentateuch.* Grand Rapids: Baker, 1982.

*Livingston, G. Herbert. *The Pentateuch in its Cultural Environment.* 2nd ed. Grand Rapids: Baker, 1987.

McCarthy, D. J. *Old Testament Covenant: A Survey of Current Opinions.* Growing Points in Theology. Atlanta: John Knox, 1972.

Nicholson, E. W. *God and His People: Covenant Theology in the Old Testament.* Oxford: Clarendon, 1986.

Noth, Martin. *Laws in the Pentateuch and Other Studies.* London: SCM, 1966.

Patrick, Dale. *Old Testament Law.* Atlanta: John Knox, 1985.

*von Rad, Gerhard. *The Problem of the Hexateuch and other Essays.* London: SCM, 1966.

*Sailhamer, John H. *The Pentateuch as Narrative: A Biblical-Theological Commentary.* Grand Rapids: Zondervan, 1992.

Suelzer, A. *The Pentateuch: A Study in Salvation History.* New York: Herder & Herder, 1964.

*Whybray, R. N. *Introduction to the Pentateuch.* Grand Rapids: Eerdmans, 1995.

Genesis

*Brueggemann, Walter. *Genesis.* Interpretation: A Bible Commentary for Teaching and Preaching. Atlanta: John Knox, 1982.

Cassuto, Umberto. *Commentary on the Book of Genesis.* 2 vols. Jerusalem: Magnes, 1961-64.

*Delitzsch, Franz. *A New Commentary on Genesis.* 2 vols. 5th ed. Edinburgh: T. &. T. Clark, 1899.

Driver, Samuel Rolles. *The Book of Genesis.* Westminster Commentaries. London: Methuen, 1904.

Fokkelman, J. P. *Narrative Art in Genesis: Specimens of Stylistic and Structural Analysis.* Assen, Netherlands: van Gorcum, 1975.

*Hamilton, Victor P. *The Book of Genesis: Chapters 1-17.* New International Commentary on the Old Testament. Grand Rapids: Eerdmans, 1990.

*———. *The Book of Genesis: Chapters 18-50.* New International Commentary on the Old Testament. Grand Rapids: Eerdmans, 1995.

Kidner, Derek. *Genesis: An Introduction and Commentary.* Tyndale Old Testament Commentaries. Downers Grove, IL: InterVarsity, 1967.

*von Rad, Gerhard. *Genesis: A Commentary.* Rev. ed. Old Testament Library. Philadelphia: Westminster, 1972.

Sarna, Nahum. *Understanding Genesis.* New York: McGraw-Hill, 1966.

Skinner, John. *A Critical and Exegetical Commentary on the Book of Genesis.* 2nd ed. International Critical Commentary. Edinburgh: T. &. T. Clark, 1930.

Speiser, Ephraim A. *Genesis.* Anchor Bible. Garden City, NY: Doubleday, 1964.

Spurrell, George J. *Notes on the Hebrew Text of the Book of Genesis.* 2nd ed. London: Frowde, 1896.

*Wenham, Gordon J. *Genesis 1-15.* Word Biblical Commentary. Waco, TX: Word, 1987.

*———. *Genesis 16-50.* Word Biblical Commentary. Dallas: Word, 1994.

Westermann, Claus. *Genesis: A Commentary.* 3 vols. Minneapolis: Augsburg, 1984-86. (see one-volume abridgement below)

———. *Genesis.* Text and Interpretation: A Practical Commentary. Grand Rapids: Eerdmans, 1987.

(Note especially Calvin on Genesis)

Exodus

Cassuto, Umberto. *A Commentary on the Book of Exodus.* Jerusalem: Magnes, 1967.

*Childs, Brevard S. *The Book of Exodus: A Critical, Theological Commentary.* Old Testament Library. Philadelphia: Westminster, 1974.

Clements, Ronald E. *Exodus.* Cambridge Bible Commentary. Cambridge: University Press, 1972.

Cole, Robert A. *Exodus.* Tyndale Old Testament Commentaries. Downers Grove, IL: InterVarsity, 1973.

*Driver, S. R. *The Book of Exodus.* Cambridge Bible for Schools and Colleges. Cambridge: Cambridge University Press, 1911.

*Durham, John I. *Exodus.* Word Biblical Commentary. Waco, TX: Word, 1987.

*Fretheim, Terence E. *Exodus.* Interpretation: A Bible Commentary for Teaching and Preaching. Louisville: Westminster/John Knox, 1991.

*Gowan, Donald E. *Theology in Exodus: Biblical Theology in the Form of a Commentary.* Philadelphia: Westminster, 1994.

Meyer, Lester. *The Message of Exodus: A Theological Commentary.* Minneapolis: Augsburg, 1983.

Noth, Martin. *Exodus.* Old Testament Library. Philadelphia: Westminster, 1962.

Sarna, Nahum. *Exploring Exodus: The Heritage of Biblical Israel.* New York: Schocken, 1986.

Leviticus

*Bonar, A. A. *A Commentary on the Book of Leviticus: Expository and Practical.* 2nd ed. London: Nisbet, 1847.

*Harrison, R. K. *Leviticus.* Tyndale Old Testament Commentaries. Downers Grove, IL: InterVarsity, 1980.

*Hartley, John E. *Leviticus.* Word Biblical Commentary. Dallas: Word, 1992.

Kellogg, S. H. *The Book of Leviticus.* 3rd ed. New York: A. C. Armstrong, 1899; reprint, Minneapolis: Klock & Klock, 1978.

Mays, James Luther. *The Book of Leviticus-The Book of Numbers.* Layman's Bible Commentary. Atlanta: John Knox, 1963.

Milgrom, Jacob. *Leviticus 1-16.* Anchor Bible. New York: Doubleday, 1991.

Noth, Martin. *Leviticus: A Commentary.* Rev. ed. Old Testament Library. Philadelphia: Westminster, 1977.

*Wenham, Gordon J. *The Book of Leviticus.* New International Commentary on the Old Testament. Grand Rapids: Eerdmans, 1979.

Numbers (see also under Leviticus)

*Ashley, Timothy R. *The Book of Numbers.* New International
    Commentary on the Old Testament. Grand Rapids: Eerdmans,
    1993.

*Budd, Philip J. *Numbers.* Word Biblical Commentary. Waco: TX,
    1984.

Gray, George B. *A Critical and Exegetical Commentary on Numbers.*
    International Critical Commentary. Edinburgh: T. &. T. Clark,
    1903.

Levine, Baruch A. *Numbers 1-20.* Anchor Bible. New York:
    Doubleday, 1993.

*Maarsingh, B. *Numbers.* Text and Interpretation: A Practical
    Commentary. Grand Rapids: Eerdmans, 1987.

Olson, Dennis T. *The Death of the Old and the Birth of the New: The
    Framework of the Book of Numbers and the Pentateuch.* Brown Judaic
    Studies, no. 71. Chico, CA: Scholars, 1985.

Riggans, Walter. *Numbers.* Daily Study Bible. Philadelphia:
    Westminster, 1983.

*Wenham, Gordon. *Numbers.* Tyndale Old Testament Commentaries.
    Downers Grove, IL: InterVarsity, 1981.

Deuteronomy

Christensen, Duane. *Deuteronomy 1-11.* Word Biblical Commentary.
    Dallas: Word, 1991.

*Clements, Ronald E. *God's Chosen People: A Theological Interpretation
    of the Book of Deuteronomy.* London: SCM, 1968.

*Craigie, Peter C. *The Book of Deuteronomy.* New International
    Commentary on the Old Testament. Grand Rapids: Eerdmans,
    1976.

*Driver, Samuel Rolles. *A Critical and Exegetical Commentary on Deuteronomy.* International Critical Commentary. Edinburgh: T. &. T. Clark, 1895.

McConville, J. Gordon. *Grace in the End: A Study in Deuteronomic Theology.* Studies in Old Testament Biblical Theology. Grand Rapids: Zondervan, 1993.

*Miller, Patrick D., Jr. *Deuteronomy.* Interpretation: A Bible Commentary for Teaching and Preaching. Louisville: Westminster/John Knox, 1990.

Nicholson, E.W. *Deuteronomy and Tradition.* Oxford: University Press, 1967.

Olson, Dennis T. *Deuteronomy and the Death of Moses.* Overtures to Biblical Theology. Philadelphia: Fortress, 1994.

*von Rad, Gerhard. *Deuteronomy.* Old Testament Library. Philadelphia: Westminster, 1966.

———. *Studies in Deuteronomy.* Studies in Biblical Theology, no. 9. London: SCM, 1953.

Smith, George Adam. *The Book of Deuteronomy.* Cambridge Bible for Schools and Colleges. Cambridge: Cambridge University Press, 1918.

Thompson, J. A. *Deuteronomy.* Tyndale Old Testament Commentaries. Downers Gove, IL: InterVarsity, 1974.

Welch, Adam Cleghorn. *Deuteronomy: The Framework to the Code.* London: Oxford University Press, 1932.

———. *The Code of Deuteronomy: A New Theory of its Origins.* London: James Clarke, 1924.

The Former Prophets: General Works (see also under The Pentateuch, General Works)

*Fretheim, Terence E. *Deuteronomic History.* Interpreting Biblical Texts. Nashville: Abingdon, 1983.

Gerbrandt, Gerald Eddie *Kingship according to the Deuteronomistic History.* Society of Biblical Literature Dissertation Series, no. 87. Atlanta: Scholars, 1986.

*Noth, Martin. *The Deuteronomistic History.* Journal for the Study of the Old Testament Supplement Series, no. 15. Sheffield: JSOT, 1981.

Polzin, Robert. *Moses and the Deuteronomist: A Literary Study of the Deuteronomic History.* New York: Seabury, 1980.

*Rast, Walter E. *Joshua, Judges, Samuel, Kings.* Proclamation Commentaries. Philadelphia: Fortress, 1978.

Weinfeld, Moshe. *Deuteronomy and the Deuteronomistic School.* Oxford: Clarendon, 1972.

Joshua

*Auld, A. Graeme. *Joshua, Judges, and Ruth.* Daily Study Bible. Philadelphia: Westminster, 1984.

Boling, Robert G., and Wright, G. Ernest. *Joshua.* Anchor Bible. Garden City, NY: Doubleday, 1982.

*Butler, Trent C. *Joshua.* Word Biblical Commentary. Waco, TX: Word, 1983.

Gray, John. *Joshua, Judges, and Ruth.* Rev. ed. New Century Bible. Grand Rapids: Eerdmans, 1986.

Hamlin, E. John. *Joshua: Inheriting the Land.* International Theological Commentary. Grand Rapids: Eerdmans, 1983.

Hawk, L. Daniel. *Every Promise Fulfilled: Contesting Plots in Joshua.* Literary Currents in Biblical Interpretation. Louisville: Westminster/John Knox, 1991.

Soggin, J. Alberto. *Joshua.* Old Testament Library. Philadelphia: Westminster, 1972.

*Woudstra, M. H. *The Book of Joshua.* New International Commentary on the Old Testament. Grand Rapids: Eerdmans, 1981.

Judges (see also under Joshua)

*Adar, Zvi. *The Biblical Narrative.* Jerusalem: Department of Education and Cultures of the World Zionist Organization, 1959.

Boling, Robert G. *Judges.* Anchor Bible. Garden City, NY: Doubleday, 1975.

*Buber, Martin. *The Kingship of God.* New York: Harper & Row, 1967.

Burney, C. F. *Judges and Kings.* 2nd ed. London: Rivingtons, 1919.

*Cundall, Arthur E., and Morris, Leon. *Judges and Ruth: An Introduction and Commentary.* Tyndale Old Testament Commentaries. Downers Grove: InterVarsity, 1968.

Hamlin, E. John. *Judges: At Risk in the Promised Land.* International Theological Commentary. Grand Rapids: Eerdmans, 1990.

Klein, Lillian R. *The Triumph of Irony in the Book of Judges.* Journal for the Study of the Old Testament Supplement Series, no. 68. Sheffield: Almond, 1988.

*Lindars, Barnabas. *Judges 1-5.* Edited by A. D. H. Mayes. Edinburgh: T. & T. Clark, 1995.

Moore, George Foot. *A Critical and Exegetical Commentary on Judges.* International Critical Commentary. Edinburgh: T. & T. Clark, 1895.

Soggin, J. Alberto. *Judges: A Commentary.* Old Testament Library. Louisville: Westminster/John Knox, 1981.

*Webb, Barry G. *The Book of Judges: An Integrated Reading.* Journal for the Study of the Old Testament Supplement Series, no. 46. Sheffield: JSOT, 1987.

(See also P. Cassell in Lange's *Commentary*)

Ruth (see also under Joshua, and Judges)

*Campbell, Edward F. *Ruth.* Anchor Bible. Garden City, NY: Doubleday, 1975.

Cooke, George Albert. *The Book of Ruth.* Rev. ed. Cambridge Bible. Cambridge: Cambridge University Press, 1913.

*Hals, Ronald M. *The Theology of the Book of Ruth.* Facet Books. Philadelphia: Fortress, 1966.

*Hubbard, Robert L., Jr. *The Book of Ruth.* New International Commentary on the Old Testament. Grand Rapids: Eerdmans, 1988.

Knight, George A. F. *Ruth and Jonah.* Torch Bible Commentaries. London: SCM, 1966.

Sasson, J. M. *Ruth: A New Translation with a Philological Commentary and a Formalist-Folklorist Interpretation.* The Johns Hopkins Near Eastern Studies. Baltimore: Johns Hopkins University Press, 1979.

Books of Samuel

Ackroyd, Peter R. *The First Book of Samuel.* Cambridge Bible Commentary on the New English Bible. Cambridge: Cambridge University Press, 1971.

———. *The Second Book of Samuel.* Cambridge Bible Commentary on the New English Bible. Cambridge: Cambridge University Press, 1977.

Anderson, Arnold. *2 Samuel.* Word Biblical Commentary. Waco, TX: Word, 1989.

*Baldwin, Joyce G. *1 and 2 Samuel.* Tyndale Old Testament Commentaries. Downers Grove, IL: InterVarsity, 1988.

*Brueggemann, Walter. *First and Second Samuel.* Interpretation: A Bible Commentary for Teaching and Preaching. Louisville: Westminster/John Knox, 1990.

*Brueggemann, Walter. *David's Truth in Israel's Imagination and Memory*. Philadelphia: Fortress, 1985.

Carlson, R. A. *David, the Chosen King*. Stockholm: Almquist and Wiksell, 1964.

*Fokkelman, J. P. *Narrative Art and Poetry in the Books of Samuel: A Full Interpretation Based on Stylistic and Structural Analyses*. 4 vols. Studia Semitica Neerlandica. Winona Lake, IN: Eisenbrauns, 1981-1993.

*Gunn, David M. *The Fate of King Saul: An Interpretation of a Biblical Story*. Journal for the Study of the Old Testament Supplement Series, no. 14. Sheffield: JSOT, 1980.

*———. *The Story of King David: Genre and Interpretation*. Journal for the Study of the Old Testament Supplement Series, no. 6. Sheffield: JSOT, 1978.

*Hertzberg, Hans Wilhelm. *I & II Samuel: A Commentary*. Old Testament Library. Philadelphia: Westminster, 1964.

*Klein, Ralph W. *1 Samuel*. Word Biblical Commentary. Waco, TX: Word, 1983.

*McCarter, P. Kyle. *1 Samuel*. Anchor Bible. Garden City, NY: Doubleday, 1980.

*———. *2 Samuel*. Anchor Bible. Garden City, NY: Doubleday, 1984.

Payne, David F. *I & II Samuel*. Daily Study Bible. Philadelphia: Westminster, 1982.

Polzin, Robert. *David and the Deuteronomist: 2 Samuel*. Indiana Studies in Biblical Literature. Bloomington, IN: University of Indiana Press, 1993.

———. *Samuel and the Deuteronomist*. San Francisco: Harper & Row, 1989.

Smith, Henry Preserved. *A Critical and Exegetical Commentary on the Books of Samuel*. International Critical Commentary. Edinburgh: T. & T. Clark, 1899.

*Welch, Adam Cleghorn. *Kings and Prophets of Israel.* London:
Lutterworth, 1952.

(See also W. G. Balkie in *The Expositor's Bible*)

Books of Kings (see also under Books of Samuel)

*Auld, A. Graeme. *I and II Kings.* Daily Study Bible. Philadelphia:
Westminster, 1986.

Burney, C. F. *Notes on the Hebrew Text of the Books of Kings.* Oxford:
Clarendon, 1903.

DeVries, Simon J. *1 Kings.* Word Biblical Commentary. Waco, TX:
Word, 1985.

*Ellul, Jacques. *The Politics of God and the Politics of Man.* Grand
Rapids: Eerdmans, 1972.

Gray, John. *I & II Kings: A Commentary.* Rev. ed. Old Testament
Library. Philadelphia: Westminster, 1970.

*Hobbs, T. R. *2 Kings.* Word Biblical Commentary. Waco, TX: Word,
1985.

Jones, G. H. *1 and 2 Kings.* 2 vols. New Century Bible Commentary.
Grand Rapids: Eerdmans, 1984.

Long, Burke O. *1 Kings, with an Introduction to Historical Literature.*
The Forms of the Old Testament Literature, vol. IX. Grand
Rapids: Eerdmans, 1984.

———. *2 Kings.* The Forms of the Old Testament Literature, vol. X.
Grand Rapids: Eerdmans, 1991.

McKenzie, Steven L. *The Trouble with Kings: The Composition of the
Book of Kings in the Deuteronomistic History.* Leiden: Brill, 1991.

Montgomery, James A., and Gehman, Henry Snyder. *A Critical and
Exegetical Commentary on the Books of Kings.* International Critical
Commentary. Edinburgh: T. & T. Clark, 1951.

*Nelson, Richard. *First and Second Kings.* Interpretation: A Bible Commentary for Teaching and Preaching. Atlanta: John Knox, 1987.

Skinner, John. *Kings.* Century Bible. Edinburgh: T. C. & E. C. Jack, 1904.

*Wiseman, Donald J. *1 & 2 Kings.* Tyndale Old Testament Commentaries. Downers Grove, IL: InterVarsity, 1993.

Books of Chronicles

Ackroyd, Peter R. *I and II Chronicles, Ezra, Nehemiah.* Torch Bible Commentaries. London: SCM, 1973.

———. *The Chronicler in His Age.* Journal for the Study of the Old Testament Supplement Series, no. 101. Sheffield: JSOT, 1991.

*Braun, Roddy. *1 Chronicles.* Word Biblical Commentary. Waco, TX: Word, 1986.

Curtis, Edward Lewis, and Madsen, Albert Alonzo. *A Critical and Exegetical Commentary on the Books of Chronicles.* International Critical Commentary. Edinburgh: T. & T. Clark, 1910.

*Dillard, Raymond B. *2 Chronicles.* Word Biblical Commentary. Waco, TX: Word, 1987.

*Japhet, Sara. *1 & 2 Chronicles: A Commentary.* Old Testament Library. Louisville: Westminster/John Knox, 1993.

Myers, Jacob M. *I Chronicles.* Anchor Bible. Garden City, NY: Doubleday, 1965.

———. *2 Chronicles.* Anchor Bible. Garden City, NY: Doubleday, 1965.

Noth, Martin. *The Chronicler's History.* Journal for the Study of the Old Testament Supplement Series, no. 50. Sheffield: JSOT Press, 1987.

Selman, Martin J. *1 & 2 Chronicles: An Introduction and Commentary.* Tyndale Old Testament Commentaries. Downers Grove, IL: InterVarsity, 1994.

*Williamson, H. G. M. *I and II Chronicles*. New Century Bible. Grand Rapids: Eerdmans, 1982.

Ezra and Nehemiah

Batten, Loring W. *A Critical and Exegetical Commentary on the Books of Ezra and Nehemiah*. International Critical Commentary. Edinburgh: T. & T. Clark, 1913.

*Blenkinsopp, Joseph. *Ezra-Nehemiah: A Commentary*. Old Testament Library. Louisville: Westminster/John Knox, 1988.

Clines, D. J. *Ezra, Nehemiah, Esther*. New Century Bible. Grand Rapids: Eerdmans, 1984.

*Fensham, F. Charles. *The Books of Ezra and Nehemiah*. New International Commentary on the Old Testament. Grand Rapids: Eerdmans, 1982.

*Kidner, Derek. *Ezra and Nehemiah*. Tyndale Old Testament Commentaries. Downers Grove: InterVarsity, 1979.

McConville, J. G. *Ezra, Nehemiah, and Esther*. Daily Study Bible. Philadelphia: Westminster, 1985.

Myers, Jacob M. *Ezra, Nehemiah*. Anchor Bible. Garden City, NY: Doubleday, 1965.

*Throntveit, Mark A. *Ezra-Nehemiah*. Interpretation: A Bible Commentary for Teaching and Preaching. Louisville: Westminster/John Knox, 1992.

*Williamson, H. G. M. *Ezra, Nehemiah*. Word Biblical Commentary. Waco, TX: Word, 1985.

Esther (see also under Ezra and Nehemiah)

*Baldwin, Joyce G. *Esther*. Tyndale Old Testament Commentaries. Downers Grove: InterVarsity, 1984.

Berg, Sandra Beth. *The Book of Esther: Motifs, Themes, and Structure.* Society of Biblical Literature Dissertation Series, no. 44. Missoula, MT: Scholars, 1979.

*Moore, Carey A. *Esther.* Anchor Bible. Garden City, NY: Doubleday, 1971.

Paton, Lewis B. *Critical and Exegetical Commentary on the Book of Esther.* International Critical Commentary. Edinburgh: T.& T. Clark, 1908.

Wisdom Literature: General Works

*Bergant, Dianne. *What are they Saying about Wisdom Literature?* New York: Paulist, 1984.

*Blenkinsopp, Joseph. *Wisdom and Law in the Ordering of Life in Israel and Early Judaism.* London: Oxford, 1983.

Brueggemann, Walter. *In Man We Trust: The Neglected Side of Biblical Faith.* Richmond: John Knox, 1972.

Clements, Ronald E. *Wisdom for a Changing World: Wisdom in Old Testament Theology.* Sheffield, BIBAL, 1990.

*Crenshaw, James L. *Old Testament Wisdom: An Introduction.* Atlanta: John Knox, 1981.

*Murphy, Roland E. *The Tree of Life: An Exploration of Biblical Wisdom Literature.* Anchor Bible Reference Library. New York: Doubleday, 1990.

Noth, Martin, and Thomas, D. W., eds. *Wisdom in Israel and in the Ancient Near East.* Vetus Testamentum Supplement, no. 3. Leiden: Brill, 1953.

Perdue, Leo G. *Wisdom and Creation: The Theology of the Wisdom Literature.* Nashville: Abingdon, 1994.

*von Rad, Gerhard. *Wisdom in Israel.* Nashville: Abingdon, 1972.

Scott, R. B. Y. *The Way of Wisdom in the Old Testament.* New York: Macmillan, 1971.

Whybray, R. N. *The Intellectual Tradition in the Old Testament.* Berlin: DeGruyter, 1974.

Job

*Anderson, Francis I. *Job.* Tyndale Old Testament Commentaries. Downers Grove, IL: InterVarsity, 1976.

*Clines, David J. A. *Job 1-20.* Word Biblical Commentary. Dallas: Word, 1990.

Dhorme, Edouard Paul. *A Commentary on the Book of Job.* London: T. Nelson, 1967; reprint, Nashville: Nelson, 1984.

Gordis, Robert. *The Book of Job.* New York: Jewish Theological Seminary of America, 1978.

*Habel, Norman C. *The Book of Job: A Commentary.* Old Testament Library. Louisville: Westminster/John Knox, 1985.

*Hartley, John E. *Job.* New International Commentary on the Old Testament. Grand Rapids: Eerdmans, 1988.

*Janzen, J. Gerald. *Job.* Interpretation: A Bible Commentary for Teaching and Preaching. Louisville: Westminster/John Knox, 1985.

Pope, Marvin H. *Job.* Anchor Bible. Garden City, NY: Doubleday, 1965.

Rowley, H. H. *Job.* Rev. ed. New Century Bible Commentary. Grand Rapids: Eerdmans, 1980.

Simundson, Daniel J. *The Message of Job: A Theological Commentary.* Minneapolis: Augsburg, 1985.

*Westermann, Claus. *The Structure of the Book of Job: A Form-Critical Analysis.* Philadelphia: Fortress, 1981.

Psalms

*Allen, Leslie C. *Psalms 101-150*. Word Biblical Commentary. Waco, TX: Word, 1983.

Anderson, Bernhard W. *Out of the Depths: The Psalms Speak for Us Today*. Philadelphia: Westminster, 1974.

Briggs, C. A., and Briggs, E. G. *A Critical and Exegetical Commentary on the Book of Psalms*. The International Critical Commentary. 2 vols. Edinburgh: T. & T. Clark, 1906-1907.

Brueggemann, Walter. *The Message of the Psalms*. Minneapolis: Augsburg, 1984.

*Craigie, Peter C. *Psalms 1-50*. Word Biblical Commentary. Waco, TX: Word, 1983.

Dahood, Mitchell. *Psalms 1-50*. Anchor Bible. Garden City, NY: Doubleday, 1965.

———. *Psalms 51-100*. Anchor Bible. Garden City, NY: Doubleday, 1968.

———. *Psalms 101-150*. Anchor Bible. Garden City, NY: Doubleday, 1970.

*Gunkel, Hermann. *The Psalms: A Form-Critical Introduction*. Facet Books Biblical Series, no. 19. Philadelphia: Fortress, 1967.

*Holladay, William L. *The Psalms Through Three Thousand Years: Prayerbook of a Cloud of Witnesses*. Philadelphia: Fortress, 1993.

*Kidner, Derek. *Psalms 1-72: An Introduction and Commentary*. Tyndale Old Testament Commentaries. Downers Grove, IL: InterVarsity, 1975.

*———. *Psalms 73-150: A Commentary*. Tyndale Old Testament Commentaries. Downers Grove, IL: InterVarsity, 1975.

*Kirkpatrick, A. F. *The Book of Psalms*. Cambridge: Cambridge University Press, 1910.

*Kraus, Hans-Joachim. *Psalms 1-59: A Commentary.* Minneapolis: Augsburg, 1988.

*———. *Psalms 60-150: A Commentary.* Minneapolis: Augsburg, 1989.

*———. *Theology of the Psalms.* Minneapolis: Augsburg, 1986.

*Mays, James Luther. *Psalms.* Interpretation: A Bible Commentary for Teaching and Preaching. Louisville: Westminster/John Knox, 1994.

*———. *The Lord Reigns: A Theological Handbook to the Psalms.* Philadelphia: Westminster, 1994.

McCann, J. Clinton, Jr. *A Theological Introduction to the Book of Psalms.* Nashville: Abingdon, 1994.

———, ed. *The Shape and Shaping of the Psalter.* Journal for the Study of the Old Testament Supplement Series, no. 159. Sheffield: JSOT, 1993.

Miller, Patrick D., Jr. *Interpreting the Psalms.* Philadelphia: Fortress, 1986.

Mowinkel, Sigmund. *The Psalms in Israel's Worship.* 2 vols. Nashville: Abingdon, 1963.

Perowne, John. *The Book of Psalms.* London: D. Ball, 1878-1879; reprint, Grand Rapids: Zondervan, 1976.

*Tate, Marvin. *Psalms 51-100.* Word Biblical Commentary. Dallas: 1990.

Weiser, Artur. *The Psalms.* Old Testament Library. Philadelphia: Westminster, 1962.

*———. *The Psalms: Structure, Content, and Message.* Minneapolis: Augsburg, 1990.

(see also Alexander Maclaren in *The Expositor's Bible*)

Proverbs

*Kidner, Derek. *Proverbs.* Tyndale Old Testament Commentaries. Downers Grove, IL: InterVarsity, 1964.

McKane, William. *Proverbs.* Old Testament Library. Philadelphia: Westminster, 1970.

*Oesterley, William O. E. *The Book of Proverbs.* Westminster Commentaries. London: Methuen, 1929.

Scott, R. B. Y. *Proverbs and Ecclesiastes.* Anchor Bible. Garden City, NY: Doubleday, 1965.

*Westermann, Claus. *Roots of Wisdom: The Oldest Proverbs of Israel and Other Peoples.* Louisville: Westminster, 1995.

*Whybray, R. N. *Proverbs.* New Century Bible Commentary. Grand Rapids: Eerdmans, 1994.

Ecclesiastes (see also under Proverbs, and Song of Solomon)

Barton, George A. *A Critical and Exegetical Commentary on the Book of Ecclesiastes.* International Critical Commentary. Edinburgh: T. & T. Clark, 1908.

*Crenshaw, James L. *Ecclesiastes: A Commentary.* Old Testament Library. Louisville: Westminster/John Knox, 1987.

Ellul, Jacques. *Reason for Being: A Meditation on Ecclesiastes.* Grand Rapids: Eerdmans, 1990.

*Gordis, Robert. *Koheleth: The Man and His World.* New York: Block, 1955.

*Murphy, Roland E. *Ecclesiastes.* Word Biblical Commentary. Dallas: Word, 1992.

*Plumptre, E. H. *Ecclesiastes: or the Preacher.* Cambridge Bible for Schools and Colleges. Cambridge: Cambridge University Press, 1888.

Whybray, R. N. *Ecclesiastes.* New Century Bible Commentary. Grand Rapids: Eerdmans, 1989.

Williams, Arthur Lukyn. *Ecclesiastes.* Cambridge Bible for Schools and Colleges. Cambridge: Cambridge University Press, 1922.

Song of Solomon (see also under Ecclesiastes)

Ginsburg, Christian David. *The Song of Songs and Qoheleth.* New York: Ktav, 1970. Reprint of Song of Songs (London: Longman, Brown, Green, Longmans, and Roberts, 1857); and Qoholet (London: Longman, Brown, Green, Longmans, and Roberts, 1861).

*Gordis, Robert. *The Song of Songs and Lamentations.* New York: Ktav, 1974.

Harper, Andrew. *The Song of Songs.* Cambridge Bible for Schools and Colleges. Cambridge: Cambridge University Press, 1912.

*Keel, Othmar. *The Song of Songs.* Philadelphia: Fortress, 1994.

Knight, George A. F. *Esther, Song of Songs, Lamentations.* Torch Bible Commentaries. London: SCM, 1955.

*Murphy, Roland E. *The Song of Songs.* Hermeneia: A Critical and Historical Commentary on the Bible. Philadelphia: Fortress, 1990.

*Pope, Marvin H. *Song of Songs.* Anchor Bible. Garden City, NY: Doubleday, 1977.

Prophetic Literature: General Works

*Blenkinsopp, Joseph. *A History of Prophecy in Israel: From the Settlement in the Land to the Hellenistic Period.* Atlanta: John Knox, 1983.

*Heschel, Abraham. *The Prophets.* 2 vols. New York: Harper, 1969.

Johnson, Aubrey R. *The Cultic Prophet in Ancient Israel.* Cardiff: University of Wales, 1962.

*Koch, Klaus. *The Prophets.* 2 vols. Philadelphia: Fortress, 1982, 1983.

*Lindblom, Johannes. *Prophecy in Ancient Israel.* Oxford: Blackwell, 1962.

*Mays, James Luther, and Achtemeier, Paul J., eds. *Interpreting the Prophets.* Philadelphia: Fortress, 1987.

Petersen, David L., ed. *Prophecy in Israel.* Issues in Religion and Theology, no. 10. Philadelphia: Fortress, 1987.

*von Rad, Gerhard. *The Message of the Prophets.* London: SCM, 1968.

Robinson, T. H. *Prophecy and Prophets in Ancient Israel.* 2nd ed. London: Duckworth, 1953.

Scott, R. B. Y. *The Relevance of the Prophets.* Rev. ed. New York: Macmillan, 1968.

*Westermann, Claus. *Basic Forms of Prophetic Speech.* Philadelphia: Westminster, 1991.

Wilson, Robert R. *Prophecy and Society in Ancient Israel.* Philadelphia: Fortress, 1980.

Young, Edward J. *My Servants the Prophets.* Grand Rapids: Eerdmans, 1952.

Isaiah

*Achtemeier, Elizabeth. *The Community and Message of Isaiah 55-66: A Theological Commentary.* Minneapolis: Augsburg, 1982.

*Alexander, Joseph A. *Prophecies of Isaiah: Earlier and Later.* London: Collins, 1848; reprint [Commentary on the Prophecies of Isaiah], Grand Rapids: Zondervan, 1953.

Clements, Ronald E. *Isaiah 1-39.* New Century Bible Commentary. Grand Rapids: Eerdmans, 1981.

*Conrad, Edgar W. *Reading Isaiah.* Overtures to Biblical Theology. Philadelphia: Fortress, 1991.

*Hayes, John H. *Isaiah, the Eighth Century Prophet: His Times & His Preaching.* Nashville: Abingdon, 1987.

Kaiser, Otto. *Isaiah 1-12: A Commentary.* 2nd ed. Old Testament Library. Philadelphia: Westminster, 1983.

———. *Isaiah 13-39: A Commentary.* Old Testament Library. Philadelphia: Westminster, 1974.

Kissane, Edward J. *The Book of Isaiah.* 2 vols. Dublin: Brown & Nolan, 1941.

Motyer, James A. *The Prophecy of Isaiah: An Introduction & Commentary.* Downers Grove, IL: InterVarsity, 1993.

*Oswalt, John N. *The Book of Isaiah: Chapters 1-39.* New International Commentary on the Old Testament. Grand Rapids: Eerdmans, 1986.

Schmitt, John J. *Isaiah and His Interpreters.* New York: Paulist, 1986.

*Seitz, Christopher R. *Isaiah 1-39.* Interpretation: A Bible Commentary for Teaching and Preaching. Louisville: Westminster/John Knox, 1993.

*———., ed. *Reading and Preaching the Book of Isaiah.* Philadelphia: Fortress, 1988.

Skinner, John. *The Book of the Prophet Isaiah.* 2 vols. Cambridge Bible for Schools and Colleges. Cambridge: Cambridge University Press, 1910, 1915.

*Watts, John D. W. *Isaiah 1-33.* Word Biblical Commentary. Waco, TX: Word, 1985.

*———. *Isaiah 34-66.* Word Biblical Commentary. Waco, TX: Word, 1987.

Westermann, Claus. *Isaiah 40-66.* Old Testament Library. Philadelphia: Westminster, 1969.

Wildberger, Hans. *Isaiah 1-12: A Commentary.* Philadelphia: Augsburg, 1991.

(see also George Adam Smith in *The Expositor's Bible*)

Jeremiah

Bright, John. *Jeremiah.* Anchor Bible. Garden City, NY: Doubleday, 1965.

Brueggemann, Walter. *To Pluck Up, To Tear Down: A Commentary on the Book of Jeremiah 1-24.* Grand Rapids: Eerdmans, 1988.

Carroll, Robert P. *Jeremiah: A Commentary.* Old Testament Library. Philadelphia: Westminster, 1986.

*Clements, Ronald E. *Jeremiah.* Interpretation: A Bible Commentary for Teaching and Preaching. Atlanta: John Knox, 1988.

*Craigie, Peter; Page, Kelly; and Drinkard, Joel. *Jeremiah 1-25.* Word Biblical Commentary. Dallas: Word, 1991.

Harrison, R. K. *Jeremiah & Lamentations.* Tyndale Old Testament Commentaries. Downers Grove, IL: InterVarsity, 1973.

*Holladay, William L. *Jeremiah 1. A Commentary on the Prophet Jeremiah Chapters 1-25.* Hermeneia: A Critical and Historical Commentary on the Bible. Philadelphia: Fortress, 1986.

*———. *Jeremiah 2. A Commentary on the Prophet Jeremiah Chapters 26-52.* Hermeneia: A Critical and Historical Commentary on the Bible. Philadelphia: Fortress, 1989.

King, Philip. *Jeremiah: An Archaeological Companion.* Philadelphia: Westminster, 1993.

McConville, J. Gordon. *Judgment and Promise: An Interpretation of the Book of Jeremiah.* Winona Lake, IN: Eisenbrauns, 1994.

*McKane, William. *A Critical and Exegetical Commentary on the Book of Jeremiah.* 2 vols. International Critical Commentary. Edinburgh: T. & T. Clark, 1988. (volume I is currently available.)

Nicholson, E. W. *Preaching to the Exiles.* Oxford: Oxford University Press, 1970.

Peake, Arthur Samuel. *Jeremiah and Lamentations.* 2 vols. Century Bible. London: Nelson, n.d.

Skinner, John. *Prophecy and Religion.* Cambridge: Cambridge University Press, 1922.

Smith, George Adam. *Jeremiah.* 4th ed. New York: Doubleday, 1929.

*Thompson, John A. *The Book of Jeremiah.* New International Commentary on the Old Testament. Grand Rapids: Eerdmans, 1980.

Welch, Adam Cleghorn. *Jeremiah: His Time and His Work.* Oxford: Basil Blackwell, 1951.

Lamentations (see also under Jeremiah)

Baumgartner, W. *Jeremiah's Poems of Lament.* Historic Texts and Interpreters, no. 7. Sheffield: Almond, 1988.

*Gottwald, Norman K. *Studies in the Book of Lamentations.* Naperville, IL: Allenson, 1962.

*Hillers, Delbert R. *Lamentations.* Rev. ed. Anchor Bible. New York: Doubleday, 1992.

Provain, Iain. *Lamentations.* New Century Bible Commentary. Grand Rapids: Eerdmans, 1991.

*Westermann, Claus. *Lamentations: Issues and Interpretation.* Minneapolis: Fortress, 1993.

Ezekiel (see also under Hosea)

*Allen, Leslie C. *Ezekiel 1-19.* Word Biblical Commentary. Dallas: Word, 1994.

*———. *Ezekiel 20-48.* Word Biblical Commentary. Dallas: Word, 1990.

*Blenkinsopp, Joseph. *Ezekiel.* Interpretation: A Bible Commentary for Teaching and Preaching. Louisville: Westminster/John Knox, 1990.

*Brownlee, William H. *Ezekiel 1-19.* Word Biblical Commentary. Waco, TX: Word, 1986.

Cooke, George Albert. *A Critical and Exegetical Commentary on the Book of Ezekiel.* International Critical Commentary. Edinburgh: T. & T. Clark, 1936.

Davidson, Andrew B. *The Book of the Prophet Ezekiel.* Cambridge Bible for Schools and Colleges. Cambridge: Cambridge University Press, 1916.

*Eichrodt, Walther. *Ezekiel.* Old Testament Library. Philadelphia: Westminster, 1970.

Fairbairn, Patrick. *Ezekiel and the Book of His Prophecy.* Edinburgh: T. & T. Clark, 1851; reprint [*An Exposition of Ezekiel*], Minneapolis: Klock & Klock, 1979.

*Hals, Ronald M. *Ezekiel.* The Forms of the Old Testament Literature, vol. XIX. Grand Rapids: Eerdmans, 1989.

*Taylor, John B. *Ezekiel: An Introduction and Commentary.* Tyndale Old Testament Commentaries. Downers Grove, IL: InterVarsity, 1969.

*Zimmerli, Walther. *Ezekiel 1: A Commentary on the Book of the Prophet Ezekiel Chapters 1-24.* Hermeneia: A Critical and Historical Commentary on the Bible. Philadelphia: Fortress, 1979.

*——. *Ezekiel 2: A Commentary on the Book of the Prophet Ezekiel Chapters 25-48.* Hermeneia: A Critical and Historical Commentary on the Bible. Philadelphia: Fortress, 1983.

Daniel

*Baldwin, Joyce G. *Daniel.* Tyndale Old Testament Commentaries. Downers Grove, IL: InterVarsity, 1979.

*Collins, John J. *Daniel.* Hermeneia: A Critical and Historical Commentary on the Bible. Minneapolis: Fortress, 1993.

*Driver, Samuel Rolles. *The Book of Daniel.* Cambridge Bible for Schools and Colleges. Cambridge: Cambridge University Press, 1905.

*Goldingay, John E. *Daniel.* Word Biblical Commentary. Dallas: Word, 1989.

Heaton, Eric W. *The Book of Daniel.* Torch Bible Commentaries. London: SCM, 1956.

Porteous, Norman W. *Daniel: A Commentary.* Old Testament Library. Philadelphia: Westminster, 1965.

*Russell, D. S. *Daniel.* Daily Study Bible. Philadelphia: Westminster, 1981.

*Towner, W. Sibley. *Daniel.* Interpretation: A Bible Commentary for Teaching and Preaching. Atlanta: John Knox, 1984.

Wiseman, Donald J., and Kitchen, Kenneth A., et al. *Notes on Some Problems in the Book of Daniel.* London: Tyndale, 1965.

(see also Otto Zockler in Lange's *Commentary*)

The Twelve (Minor) Prophets: General Works

*Achtemeier, Elizabeth. *Nahum-Malachi.* Interpretation: A Bible Commentary for Teaching and Preaching. Atlanta: John Knox, 1986.

*Allen, Leslie C. *The Books of Joel, Obadiah, Jonah and Micah.* New International Commentary on the Old Testament. Grand Rapids: Eerdmans, 1976.

Craigie, Peter C. *Twelve Prophets.* 2 vols. Daily Study Bible. Philadelphia: Westminster, 1984, 1985.

Driver, Samuel Rolles. *The Minor Prophets.* New York: Oxford University Press, 1904.

Eaton, John. H. *Obadiah, Nahum, Habakkuk, and Zephaniah: Introduction and Commentary.* London: SCM, 1961.

House, P. R. *The Unity of the Twelve.* Journal for the Study of the Old Testament Supplement Series, no. 97. Sheffield: Almond, 1990.

King, Philip. *Amos, Hosea, Micah: An Archaeological Commentary.* Philadelphia: Westminster, 1988.

*Limburg, James. *Hosea-Micah.* Interpretation: A Bible Commentary for Teaching and Preaching. Atlanta: John Knox, 1988.

von Orelli, Conrad. *The Twelve Minor Prophets.* Edinburgh: T. & T. Clark, 1897; reprint, Minneapolis: Klock & Klock, 1977.

*Smith, Ralph L. *Micah-Malachi.* Word Biblical Commentary. Waco, TX: Word, 1984.

*Stuart, Douglas. *Hosea-Jonah.* Word Biblical Commentary. Waco, TX: Word, 1987.

(see also George Adam Smith on the Minor Prophets in *The Expositor's Bible*)

Hosea

*Anderson, Francis I., and Freedman, David Noel. *Hosea.* Anchor Bible. Garden City, NY: Doubleday, 1980.

Hubbard, David A. *With Bands of Love.* Grand Rapids: Eerdmans, 1967.

——. *Hosea.* Tyndale Old Testament Commentaries. Downers Grove, IL: InterVarsity, 1990.

*Mays, James Luther. *Hosea: A Commentary.* Old Testament Library. Philadelphia: Westminster, 1969.

Robinson, H. Wheeler. *Two Hebrew Prophets: Studies in Hosea and Ezekiel.* London: Lutterworth, 1948; reprint, 1964.

*Ward, James M. *Hosea: A Theological Commentary.* New York: Harper & Row, 1966.

*Wolff, Hans Walter. *Hosea: A Commentary on the Book of the Prophet Hosea.* Hermeneia: A Critical and Historical Commentary on the Bible. Philadelphia: Fortress, 1974.

Joel

*Crenshaw, James L. *Joel.* Anchor Bible. New York: Doubleday, 1995.

Driver, Samuel R. *The Books of Joel and Amos.* Cambridge Bible for Schools and Colleges. Cambridge: Cambridge University Press, 1915.

Hubbard, David A. *Joel & Amos.* Tyndale Old Testament Commentaries. Downers Grove, IL: InterVarsity, 1989.

Kapelrud, Arvid. *Joel Studies.* Uppsala: Lundequistska, 1948.

*Wolff, Hans Walter. *A Commentary on the Books of the Prophets Joel and Amos.* Hermeneia: A Critical and Historical Commentary on the Bible. Philadelphia: Fortress, 1977.

Amos (see also under Joel)

*Anderson, Francis I., and Freedman, David Noel. *Amos.* Anchor Bible. New York: Doubleday, 1989.

Harper, William Rainey. *A Critical and Exegetical Commentary on Amos and Hosea*. International Critical Commentary. Edinburgh: T. & T. Clark, 1905.

*Hasel, Gerhard. *Understanding the Book of Amos: Basic Issues in the Current Interpretations*. Grand Rapids: Baker, 1991.

*Hayes, John H. *Amos, the Eighth Century Prophet: His Times & His Preaching*. Nashville: Abingdon, 1988.

Kapelrud, Arvid. *Central Ideas in Amos*. Oslo: Universitets Forlaget, 1971.

*Mays, James Luther. *Amos: A Commentary*. Old Testament Library. Philadelphia: Westminster, 1969.

Motyer, James A. *The Day of the Lion: The Message of Amos*. The Old Testament Speaks. Downers Grove, IL: InterVarsity, 1974.

*Paul, Shalom. *Amos*. Hermeneia: A Critical and Historical Commentary on the Bible. Minneapolis: Fortress, 1991.

*Watts, John D. W. *Studying the Book of Amos*. Nashville: Broadman, 1966.

Obadiah

Baker, David W. *Obadiah, Jonah, Micah*. Tyndale Old Testament Commentaries. Downers Grove: IL: InterVarsity, 1989.

Lanchester, H. C. O. *Obadiah and Jonah*. Cambridge: Cambridge University Press, 1918.

*Watts, John D. W. *Obadiah: A Critical and Exegetical Commentary*. Grand Rapids: Eerdmans, 1967.

*Wolff, Hans Walter. *Obadiah and Jonah: A Commentary*. Minneapolis: Augsburg, 1986.

Jonah (see also under Obadiah)

Bickerman, Elias. *Four Strange Books of the Bible.* New York: Shocken, 1967.

*Ellul, Jacques. *The Judgment of Jonah.* Grand Rapids: Eerdmans, 1971.

Fairbairn, Patrick. *Jonah: His Life, Character, and Mission.* Edinburgh: John Johnstone, 1849; reprint, Grand Rapids: Kregel, 1964.

*Fretheim, Terence E. *The Message of Jonah: A Theological Commentary.* Minneapolis: Augsburg, 1977.

*Hasel, Gerhard F. *Jonah: Messenger of the Eleventh Hour.* Mt. View, CA: Pacific, 1976.

Limburg, James. *Jonah: A Commentary.* Old Testament Library. Louisville: Westminster/John Knox, 1993.

Magonet, Jonathan. *Form and Meaning: Studies in the Literary Techniques in the Book of Jonah.* Bible and Literature Series, no. 8. Sheffield: Almond, 1983.

*Sasson, J. M. *Jonah.* Anchor Bible. New York: Doubleday, 1990.

(See also Trible's *Rhetorical Criticism,* under Old Testament Exegetical Method/Hermeneutics.)

Micah (see also under Obadiah)

Cheyne, T. K. *Micah.* Cambridge Bible for Schools and Colleges. Cambridge: Cambridge University Press, 1902.

Copass, B. A., and Carlson, E. L. *A Study of the Prophet Micah.* Grand Rapids: Baker, 1950.

*Hillers, Delbert R. *Micah.* Hermeneia: A Critical and Historical Commentary on the Bible. Philadelphia: Fortress, 1984.

Margolis, M. L. *The Holy Scripture with Commentary: Micah.* Philadelphia: Jewish Publication Society of America, 1908.

*Mays, James Luther. *Micah: A Commentary.* Old Testament Library. Philadelphia: Westminster, 1976.

*Wolff, Hans Walter. *Micah: A Commentary.* Minneapolis: Augsburg, 1990.

*———. *Micah the Prophet.* Philadelphia: Fortress, 1981.

Nahum, Habakkuk, and Zephaniah

Baker, David W. *Nahum, Habakkuk, Zephaniah.* Tyndale Old Testament Commentaries. Downers Grove, IL: InterVarsity, 1989.

Bennett, T. Miles. *The Books of Nahum and Zephaniah.* Grand Rapids: Baker, 1968.

*Berlin, Adele. *Zephaniah.* Anchor Bible. New York: Doubleday, 1994.

*Davidson, Andrew B. *Nahum, Habakkuk, and Zephaniah.* Cambridge Bible for Schools and Colleges. Cambridge: Cambridge University Press, 1896.

Eaton, John H. *Obadiah, Nahum, Habakkuk and Zephaniah.* Torch Bible Commentaries. London: SCM, 1961.

*Gowan, Donald E. *The Triumph of Faith in Habakkuk.* Atlanta: John Knox, 1976.

*Maier, Walter A. *The Book of Nahum: A Commentary.* St. Louis: Concordia, 1959.

*Roberts, J. J. M. *Nahum, Habakkuk, and Zephaniah: A Commentary.* Old Testament Library. Louisville: Westminster/John Knox, 1990.

Haggai, Zechariah, and Malachi

*Baldwin, Joyce G. *Haggai, Zechariah, Malachi: An Introduction and Commentary.* Tyndale Old Testament Commentaries. Downers Grove, IL: InterVarsity, 1972.

*Kaiser, Walter C., Jr. *God's Unchanging Love.* Grand Rapids: Baker, 1984.

Mason, R. A. *The Books of Haggai, Zechariah and Malachi.* Cambridge Bible Commentary. Cambridge: Cambridge University Press, 1977.

McDonald, Beth Glazier. *Malachi: The Divine Messenger.* Society of Biblical Literature Dissertation Series, no. 98. Atlanta: Scholars, 1987.

*Meyers, Carol L., and Meyers, Eric M. *Haggai, Zechariah 1-8.* Anchor Bible. New York: Doubleday, 1987.

*———. *Zechariah 9-14.* Anchor Bible. New York: Doubleday, 1993.

Oswalt, John N. *Where are You, God?* Wheaton: Victor, 1982.

Perowne, T. T. *Haggai and Zechariah.* Cambridge Bible for Schools and Colleges. Cambridge: Cambridge University Press, 1886.

*Petersen, David L. *Haggai and Zechariah 1-8: A Commentary.* Old Testament Library. Philadelphia: Westminster, 1984.

*———. *Zechariah 9-14 and Malachi: A Commentary.* Old Testament Library. Louisville: Westminster/John Knox, 1995.

*Verhoff, Pieter A. *The Books of Haggai and Malachi.* New International Commentary on the Old Testament. Grand Rapids: Eerdmans, 1987.

*Wolff, Hans Walter. *Haggai.* Minneapolis: Augsburg, 1988.

THE INTERTESTAMENTAL PERIOD

Judaism and Jewish Culture: Primary Sources (See also under Apocrypha and Pseudepigrapha of the Old Testament)

Blackman, P. *Mishnayot: Pointed Hebrew Text: English Translation, Introductions.* New York: Judaica, 1963-1964.

*Danby, Hebert. *The Mishnah.* London: Oxford University Press, 1933.

Epstein, Isidore, ed. *The Babylonian Talmud.* 18 vols. London: Soncino, 1961.

Freedman, Harry., ed. *The Midrash Rabbah.* 5 vols. London: Soncino, 1977.

*Glatzer, Norman, ed. *The Essential Philo.* New York: Schocken, 1971.

*Nickelsburg, George W. E., and Stone, Michael E. *Faith and Piety in Early Judaism: Texts and Documents.* Philadelphia: Fortress, 1983.

*Whiston, William. *The Works of Josephus.* New ed. Peabody, MA: Hendrickson, 1987.

*Young, C. D., and Scholer, David M. *The Works of Philo.* New ed. Peabody, MA: Hendrickson, 1993.

(See relevant volumes in the *Loeb Classical Library*.)

See also here the series, published by Fortress,* "Compendia Rerum Iudaicarum ad Novem Testamentum, Section Two: The Literature of the Jewish People in the Period of the Second Temple and the Talmud"

Volume 1: *Mikra: Text, Translation, Reading and Interpretation of the Hebrew Bible in Ancient Judaism and Early Christianity*, ed. Jan Martin Mulder (1988)

Volume 2: *Jewish Writings of the Second Temple Period: Apocrypha, Pseudepigra, Qumran, Sectarian Writings, Philo, Josephus,* ed. Michael E. Stone (1984)

Volume 3A: *The Literature of the Sages: Oral Tora, Halakha, Mishna, Tosefta, Talmud, External Tractates,* ed. S. Safari (1988)

Judaism and Jewish Culture: Secondary Sources (See also under New Testament History and Geography)

Bickerman, Elias. *From Ezra to the Last of the Maccabees.* New York: Schocken, 1962. Reprint of *The Jews: Their History, Culture, and Religion* (New York: Harper & Bros, 1949); and *The Maccabees: Their History from the Beginnings to the Fall of the House of the Hasmoneans* (New York: Schocken, 1947).

*Boccaccini, Gabriele. *Middle Judaism: Jewish Thought, 300 B.C.E. - 200 C. E.* Minneapolis: Fortress, 1991.

Cohen, Shaye J. D. *From the Maccabees to the Mishnah.* Library of Early Christianity. Philadelphia: Westminster, 1987.

*Daube, David. *The New Testament and Rabbinic Judaism.* London: Athlone, 1956.

*Davies, Louis W. D., and Finkelstein, Louis. *The Cambridge History of Judaism.* Cambridge: Cambridge University Press, 1984.

Dunn, James D. G. *The Partings of the Ways Between Christianity and Judaism and their Significance for the Character of Christianity.* Philadelphia: Trinity Press International, 1991.

Foerster, Werner *From the Exile to Christ: Historical Introduction to Palestinian Judaism.* Philadelphia: Fortress, 1964.

*Grant, Frederick C. *Ancient Judaism and the New Testament.* New York: Macmillan, 1959.

*Hengel, Martin. *Judaism and Hellenism: Studies in their Encounter in Palestine during the Early Hellenistic Period.* Philadelphia: Fortress, 1974.

———. *Jews, Greeks and Barbarians.* Philadelphia: Fortress, 1980.

*Kraft, Robert A., and Nickelsburg, George W. E., eds. *Early Judaism and its Modern Interpreters.* The Bible and its Modern Interpreters. Atlanta: Scholars, 1986.

Leon, Harry J. *The Jews of Ancient Rome.* Updated ed. Peabody, MA: Hendrickson, 1995.

Mason, Steve. *Josephus and the New Testament.* Peabody, MA: Hendrickson, 1995.

Moore, George Foot. *Judaism in the First Centuries of the Christian Era: The Age of the Tannaim.* 3 vols. Cambridge, MA: Harvard University Press, 1927-1930.

*Neusner, Jacob. *Foundations of Judaism.* Philadelphia: Fortress, 1988.

*———. *Introduction to Rabbinic Literature.* Anchor Bible Reference Library. New York: Doubleday, 1994.

*———. *Judaism in the Beginning of Christianity.* Philadelphia: Fortress, 1984.

———. *What is Midrash?* Guides to Biblical Scholarship. Philadelphia: Fortress, 1987.

Peters, F. E. *The Harvest of Hellenism: A History of the Near East from Alexander the Great to the Triumph of Christianity.* New York: Simon & Schuster, 1970.

Russell, D. S. *The Jews from Alexander to Herod.* London: Oxford, University Press, 1967.

*Sanders, E. P. *Judaism: Practice and Belief, 63 BCE-66 CE.* Philadelphia: Trinity Press International, 1992.

*Strack, Hermann L., and Stemberger, Günter. *Introduction to the Talmud and Midrash.* Minneapolis: Fortress, 1992.

Tcherikover, Victor. *Hellenistic Civilization and the Jews.* New York: Atheneum, 1975.

See also here the series, published by Fortress, *"Compendia Rerum Iudaicarum ad Novum Testamentum: Section Three: Jewish Traditions in Early Christian Literature"

Volume 1: *Paul and the Jewish Law: Halakha in the Letters of the Apostle to the Gentiles,* by Peter J. Tomson (1990)

Volume 2: *Jewish Historiography and Iconography in Early and Medieval Christianity,* by Heinz Schreckenberg and Kurt Schubert (1991)

Volume 3: *Philo in Early Christian Literature: A Survey,* by David T. Runia (1993)

Septuagint

Brenton, Lancelot C. L. *The Septuagint with Apocrypha: Greek and English.* London: Samuel Bagster & Sons, 1851; reprint, Grand Rapids: Zondervan, 1982.

Brock, Sebastian P.; Fritzsch, Charles T.; and Jellicoe, Sidney. *A Classified Bibliography of the LXX.* Philadelphia: Fortress, 1974.

Conybeare, F. C., and Stock, St. George. *Grammar of Septuagint Greek: With Selected Readings, Vocabularies, and Updated Indexes.* Peabody, MA: Hendrickson, 1988.

Dogniez, Cécile. *Biblicgraphy of the Septuagint: 1970 - 1993.* Vetus Testamentum Supplemats, no. 60. Leiden: Brill, 1995

Hatch, Edwin. *Essays in Biblical Greek.* Oxford: Oxford University Press, 1889.

*Hatch, Edwin, and Redpath, Henry A. *A Concordance to the Septuagint.* 2 vols. Oxford: Clarendon, 1897-1906.

*Jellicoe, S. *The Septuagint and Modern Study.* Oxford: Oxford University Press, 1968.

Klein, Ralph W. *Textual Criticism of the Old Testament: The Septuagint after Qumran.* Guides to Biblical Scholarship. Philadelphia: Fortress, 1974.

Lust, Johann; Eynikel, E.; and Hauspie, K. (with G. Chamberlin), eds.
    A Greek-English Lexicon of the Septuagint. Stuttgart: Deutsche
    Bibelgesellschaft, 1992—.
    (Volume 1 presently available; subsequent volumes will appear.)

Morrish, George. *A Concordance to the Septuagint.* Grand Rapids:
    Zondervan, 1976.

*Olofsson, Staffan. *God is My Rock: A Study of Translation Technique
    and Theological Exegesis in the Septuagint.* Stockholm: Almquist &
    Wiksell, 1990.

Rahlfs, Alfred, ed. *Septuaginta.* Stuttgart: Deutsche Bibelgesellschaft,
    1935.

*Swete, Henry Barclay. *An Introduction to the Old Testament in Greek.*
    Revised by R. R. Ottley. Cambridge: Cambridge University Press,
    1914.

——. *The Old Testament in Greek: According to the Septuagint.* 3 vols.
    Cambridge: Cambridge University Press, 1901-1905.

Taylor, Bernard A. *Analytical Lexicon to the Septuagint.* Regency
    Reference Library. Grand Rapids: Zondervan, 1994

Apocrypha and Pseudepigrapha of the Old Testament

*Charles, R. H. *The Apocrypha and Pseudepigrapha of the Old Testament
    in English: With Introductions and Critical and Explanatory Notes.* 2
    vols. Oxford: Clarendon, 1913.

*Charlesworth, James H. *The Old Testament Pseudepigrapha.* 2 vols.
    Garden City, NJ: Doubleday, 1983, 1985.

——. *The Old Testament Pseudepigrapha and the New Testament:
    Prolegomena for the Study of Christian Origins.* Cambridge:
    Cambridge University Press, 1985.

Lightfoot, J. B.; James, M. R.; Swete, H. B., et al, eds. *Excluded Books of
    the New Testament.* London: E. Nash & Grayson, 1927.

*Metzger, Bruce M. *An Introduction to the Apocrypha.* New York: Oxford University Press, 1957.

*Nickelsburg, George W. E. *Jewish Literature Between the Bible and the Mishnah: A Historical and Literary Introduction.* Philadelphia: Fortress, 1981.

Rost, Leonhard. *Judaism Outside the Hebrew Canon.* Nashville: Abingdon, 1976.

Russell, D. S. *The Old Testament Pseudepigrapha: Patriarchs & Prophets in Early Judaism.* Philadelphia: Fortress, 1987.

Torrey, Charles C. *The Apocryphal Literature: A Brief Introduction.* New Haven, CT: Yale University Press, 1945.

Qumran and the Dead Sea Scrolls

Barthelemy, D., and Milik, J. T., et al., eds. *Discoveries in the Judean Desert.* 5 vols. Oxford: Clarendon, 1955-1989.

*Charlesworth, James H. *Graphic Concordance to the Dead Sea Scrolls.* Louisville: Westminster/John Knox, 1992.

*———., ed. *Jesus and the Dead Sea Scrolls.* Anchor Bible Reference Library. New York: Doubleday, 1992.

*———, ed. *The Princeton Theological Seminary Dead Sea Scrolls Project.* 10 vols. Louisville: Westminster/John Knox, 1994—. (Volume 1 has appeared; the rest are awaited.)

Cross, Frank Moore. *Ancient Library of Qumran and Modern Biblical Studies.* Rev. ed. Garden City, NJ: Doubleday, 1961.

*Fitzmyer, Joseph A. *Dead Sea Scrolls: Major Publications and Tools for Study.* Rev. ed. Atlanta: Scholars, 1990.

*Gaster, Theodor H. *The Dead Sea Scriptures: With Introduction and Notes.* 3rd ed. Garden City, NJ: Doubleday, 1976.

*Martinez, Florentino Garcia. *The Dead Sea Scrolls Translated: The Qumran Texts in English.* Leiden: Brill, 1994.

———, and Barrera, Julio Trebolle. *The People of the Dead Sea Scrolls: Their Literature, Social Organization and Religious Beliefs.* Leiden: Brill, 1994.

*Ringgren, Helmer. *The Faith of Qumran: Theology of the Dead Sea Scrolls.* New York: Crossroad, 1992.

Shanks, Hershel, ed. *Understanding the Dead Sea Scrolls.* New York: Random House, 1992.

VanderKam, James C. *The Dead Sea Scrolls Today.* Grand Rapids: Eerdmans, 1994.

*Vermes, Geza. *The Dead Sea Scrolls in English.* 3rd ed. Sheffield: JSOT, 1987.

(See also the journal *Dead Sea Discoveries*)

Apocalyptic and Apocalypticism

Frost, S. B. *Old Testament Apocalyptic: Its Origins and Growth.* London: Epworth, 1952.

Hanson, Paul D. *The Dawn of Apocalyptic.* 2nd ed. Philadelphia: Fortress, 1979

———. *Old Testament Apocalyptic.* Interpreting Biblical Texts. Nashville: Abingdon, 1987.

*Minear, Paul S. *New Testament Apocalyptic.* Nashville: Abingdon, 1981.

Morris, Leon. *Apocalytpic.* Grand Rapids: Eerdmans, 1972.

Rowland, C. *The Open Heaven: A Study of Apocalyptic in Judaism and Early Christianity.* New York: Crossroad, 1982.

*Russell, D. S. *The Method and Message of Jewish Apocalyptic: 200 BC - AD 100.* Old Testament Library. Philadelphia: Westminster, 1964.

*Schmithals, Walter. *The Apocalyptic Movement: Introduction and Interpretation.* Nashville: Abingdon, 1975.

THE NEW TESTAMENT

Bibliographic Aids

Carson, D. A. *New Testament Commentary Survey.* 3rd. ed. Grand Rapids: Baker, 1989.

*France, R. T. *A Bibliographic Guide to New Testament Research.* Sheffield: JSOT, 1979.

*Harrington, Daniel J. *The New Testament: A Bibliography.* Wilmington, DE: Michael Glazier, 1985.

*Martin, Ralph P. *New Testament Books for Pastor and Teacher.* Philadelphia: Westminster, 1984.

Scholer, David. M. *A Basic Bibliographic Guide for New Testament Exegesis.* Grand Rapids: Eerdmans, 1973.

Periodicals

Journal for the Study of the New Testament; New Testament Abstracts; New Testament Studies; Novum Testamentum.

History of Interpretation and the Canon (See also under New Testament Introductions)

*Baird, William. *History of New Testament Research: Volume One, From Deism to Tübingen.* Minneapolis: Fortress, 1992.

*Epp, Eldon Jay, and MacRae, George W., eds. *The New Testament and its Modern Interpreters.* The Bible and Its Modern Interpreters. Philadelphia: Fortress, 1989.

Gamble, Harry Y. *The New Testament Canon: Its Making and Meaning.* Guides to Biblical Scholarship. Philadelphia: Fortress, 1985.

Harris, Horton. *The Tübingen School: A Historical and Theological Investigation of the School of F. C. Baur.* Grand Rapids: Baker, 1990.

*Kümmel, Werner Georg. *The New Testament: The History of the Investigation of its Problems.* Nashville: Abingdon, 1972.

*Metzger, Bruce M. *The Canon of the New Testament: Its Origin, Development, and Significance.* Oxford: Clarendon, 1987.

Moule, C. F. D. *The Birth of the New Testament.* Black's New Testament Commentaries. 3rd ed. San Francisco: Harper & Row, 1981.

*Neill, Stephen, and Wright, Tom. *The Interpretation of the New Testament 1861-1986.* 2nd ed. London: Oxford, 1964.

Riches, John K. *A Century of New Testament Study.* Valley Forge, PA: Trinity Press International, 1993.

Westcott, Brooke Foss. *A General Survey of the History of the Canon of the New Testament.* 7th ed. Cambridge: Macmillan, 1896.

History and Geography: Primary Sources

*Barrett, C. K., ed. *The New Testament Background: Selected Documents.* New York: Harper, 1957.

*Cartlidge, David R., and Dungan, David L., eds. *Documents for the Study of the Gospels.* Rev. ed. Minneapolis: Fortress, 1993.

Kee, Howard Clark. *The Origins of Christianity: Sources and Documents.* Englewood Cliffs, NJ: Prentice-Hall, 1973.

Layton, Bentley. *Gnostic Scriptures.* Garden City, NY: Doubleday, 1987.

Robinson, James M., ed. *The Nag Hammadi Library.* Rev. ed. San Francisco: Harper & Row, 1988.

History and Geography: Secondary Sources (See also under Intertestamental Period—Judaism and Jewish Culture)

Bevan, Edwyn. *Jerusalem Under the High Priests.* London: Arnold, 1904.

Brown, Raymond E. *The Churches the Apostles Left Behind.* New York: Paulist, 1984.

Brown, Raymond E. and Meier, John P. *Antioch and Rome: New Testament Cradles of Catholic Christianity.* New York: Paulist, 1983.

Bruce, F. F. *Men and Movements in the Primitive Church: Studies in Early non-Pauline Christianity.* Exeter: Paternoster, 1979.

*———. *New Testament History.* Garden City, NY: Doubleday, 1969.

Charlesworth, James H., ed. *The Messiah: Developments in Earliest Judaism and Christianity.* Minneapolis: Fortress, 1992.

Collins, John J. *The Scepter and the Star: The Messiahs of the Dead Sea Scrolls and Other Ancient Literature.* Anchor Bible Reference Library. New York: Doubleday, 1995.

Evans, Craig A. *Noncanonical Writings and New Testament Interpretation.* Peabody, MA: Hendrickson, 1992.

Ferguson, Everett. *Backgrounds of Early Christianity.* Grand Rapids: Eerdmans, 1987.

Goppelt, Leonhard. *Apostolic and Post-Apostolic Times.* Grand Rapids: Baker, 1977.

Hedrick, Charles, ed. *Nag Hammadi, Gnosticism & Early Christianity.* Peabody, MA: Hendrickson, 1983.

Horsley, Richard A., and Hanson, John S. *Bandits, Prophets, and Messiahs: Popular Movements at the Time of Jesus.* San Francisco: Harper, 1985.

*Jeremias, Joachim. *Jerusalem in the Time of Jesus: An Investigation into Economic and Social Conditions During the New Testament Period.* Philadelphia: Fortress, 1969.

Jonas, Hans. *The Gnostic Religions: The Message of the Alien God at the Beginnings of Christianity.* 2nd ed. Boston: Beacon, 1963.

Keener, Craig S. *The IVP Bible Background Commentary: New Testament.* Downers Grove, IL: InterVarsity, 1994.

Lohse, Eduard. *The New Testament Environment.* Nashville: Abingdon, 1976.

MacMullen, Ramsay. *Paganism in the Roman Empire.* New Haven, Yale University Press, 1981.

van der Meer, Frederik, and Mohrmann, Christine. *Atlas of the Early Christian World.* Edited by Mary F. Hedlund and H. H. Rowley. London: Nelson, 1958.

Mowinkel, Sigmund. *He That Cometh.* New York: Abingdon, 1954.

*Reicke, Bo. *The New Testament Era: The World of the Bible from 500 B.C. to A.D. 100.* Philadelphia: Fortress, 1974.

Reitzenstein, Richard. *Hellenistic Mystery-Religions: Their Basic Ideas and Significance.* Pittsburgh: Pickwick, 1977.

Roetzel, Calvin J. *The World that Shaped the New Testament.* Atlanta: John Knox, 1985.

*Schürer, Emil. *The History of the Jewish People in the Age of Jesus Christ.* 4 vols. Revised and edited by Geza Vermes, Fergus Millar, and Matthew Black. Edinburgh: T. & T. Clark, 1973-1987.

Sherwin-White, A. N. *Roman Society and Roman Law in the New Testament.* London: Oxford, 1963; reprint, Grand Rapids: Baker, 1978.

Simon, Marcel. *Jewish Sects at the Time of Jesus.* Philadelphia: Fortress, 1967.

Wilken, Robert Louis. *The Christians as the Romans Saw Them.* New Haven, CT: Yale University Press, 1984.

Wilkinson, J. *Jerusalem as Jesus Knew It.* London: Thames and Hudson, 1978.

Yamuchi, Edwin. *Harper's World of the New Testament.* San Francisco: Harper & Row, 1981.

Greek Grammars

*Blass, F., and Debrunner, A. *A Greek Grammar of the New Testament and other Early Christian Literature.* Chicago: University of Chicago Press, 1961.

*Brooks, James A., and Winbery, Carlton L. *Syntax of New Testament Greek.* Lanham, MD: University Press of America, 1979.

Burton, Ernest De Witt. *Syntax of the Moods and Tenses in New Testament Greek.* Chicago: University of Chicago Press, 1900; reprint, Grand Rapids: Kregel, 1976.

Dana, H. E., and Mantey, Julius R. *A Manual Grammar of the Greek New Testament.* New York: Macmillan, 1927.

Greenlee, J. Harold. *A Concise Exegetical Grammar of New Testament Greek.* 3rd ed. Grand Rapids: Eerdmans, 1963.

*Moule, C. F. D. *An Idiom-Book of New Testament Greek.* 2nd ed. Cambridge: Cambridge University Press, 1959.

*Moulton, James Hope; Howard, Wilbert Francis; and Turner, Nigel. *A Grammar of New Testament Greek.* 4 vols. Edinburgh: T. & T. Clark, 1976.

Owings, Timothy. *A Cumulative Index to New Testament Greek Grammars.* Grand Rapids: Baker, 1983.

*Robertson, Archibald T. *A Grammar of the Greek New Testament in the Light of Historical Research.* Nashville: Broadman, 1934.

Robertson, Archibald T., and Davis, W. Hersey. *A New Short Grammar of the Greek Testament.* 10th ed. New York: Harper & Bros., 1958; reprint, Grand Rapids: Baker, 1977.

Zerwick, Maximilian. *Biblical Greek.* Scripta Pontificii Instituti Biblici, No. 114. Rome: Pontifical Biblical Institute, 1963.

Greek Lexicons

*Abbott-Smith, G. A. *A Manual Greek Lexicon and Supplement.* Edinburgh: T. & T. Clark, 1937.

*Arndt, William F., and Gingrich, F. Wilbur. *A Greek-English Lexicon of the New Testament and other Early Christian Literature: A Translation and adaptation of Walter Bauer's Griechisch-Deutsches Worterbuch zu den Schriften des Neuen Testaments und der ubrigen urchristlichen Literatur; 2nd ed. rev. and augmented by F. Wilbur Gingrich and Frederick W. Danker from Walter Bauer's 5th ed., 1958.* Chicago: University of Chicago Press, 1979.

Kubo, Sakae. *A Reader's Greek-English Lexicon of the New Testament.* Grand Rapids: Zondervan, 1975.

Liddell, Henry George, and Scott, Robert. *A Greek-English Lexicon.* Rev. ed. Oxford: Clarendon, 1940.

Louw, Johannes P. and Nida, Eugene A. *Greek-English Lexicon of the New Testament Based on Semantic Dogmatics.* 2 vols. New York: United Bible Societies, 1988.

Moulton, Harold K. *The Analytical Greek Lexicon.* Rev. ed. Grand Rapids: Zondervan, 1978.

*Moulton, James Hope, and Milligan, George. *The Vocabulary of the Greek Testament Illustrated from the Papyri and Other Non-Literary Sources.* Grand Rapids: Eerdmans, 1930.

*Thayer, Joseph Henry. *Greek-English Lexicon of the New Testament: Being Grimm's Wilke's Clavis Novi Testamenti.* Grand Rapids: Zondervan, 1962. (Originally published in 1889)
(The edition published by Hendrickson is numerically coded to Strong's)

Theological Dictionaries (Wordbooks)

*Balz, Horst, and Schneider, Gerhard. *Exegetical Dictionary of the New Testament.* 3 vols. Grand Rapids: Eerdmans, 1990.

*Brown, Colin, ed. *The New International Dictionary of New Testament Theology.* 3 vols. Grand Rapids: Zondervan, 1975-1979.

Cremer, H. *Biblico-Theological Lexicon of New Testament Greek.* New York: Scribner's, 1895.

*Kittel, Gerhard, and Friedrich, Gerhard. *Theological Dictionary of the New Testament.* 10 vols. Grand Rapids: Eerdmans, 1964-1976.

———. *Theological Dictionary of the New Testament: Abridged in One Volume by Geoffrey W. Bromiley.* Grand Rapids: Eerdmans, 1985.

Spicq, Ceslas. *Theological Lexicon of the New Testament.* 3 vols. Peabody, MA: Hendrickson, 1994.

Turner, Nigel. *Christian Words.* Nashville: Thomas Nelson, 1981.

Concordances to the Greek New Testament

Aland, Kurt, ed. *Vollständige Konkordanz zum Griechischen Neuen Testament.* 2 vols. Berlin: de Gruyter, 1975.

Bachmann, H., and Slaby, W. A. *Computer Concordance to the Novum Testamentum Graece.* Berlin: de Gruyter, 1985.

*Moulton, W. F., and Geden, A. S. *A Concordance to the Greek Testament.* 5th ed. Edinburgh: T. & T. Clark, 1978.

*Smith, J. B. *Greek-English Concordance to the New Testament.* Scottsdale, PA: Herald, 1955.

Wigram, George V. *The Englishman's Greek Concordance of the New Testament.* 9th ed. Grand Rapids: Zondervan, 1970.

Concordances to the English New Testament

Darton, Michael. *Modern Concordance to the New Testament.* Garden City, NY: Doubleday, 1976.

*Morrison, Clinton. *An Analytical Concordance to the Revised Standard Version of the New Testament.* Philadelphia: Westminster, 1970.

Textual Criticism

*Aland, Kurt, and Aland, Barbara. *The Text of the New Testament: An Introduction to the Critical Editions and to the Theory and Practice of Modern Textual Criticism.* Grand Rapids: Eerdmans, 1987.

Colwell, Ernest Cadman. *Studies in Methodology of Textual Criticism of the New Testament.* Leiden: Brill, 1969.

Ehrman, Bart D., and Holmes, Michael W., eds. *The Text of the New Testament in Contemporary Research: Essays on the Status Quaestionis.* Grand Rapids: Eerdmans, 1995.

*Epp, Eldon J., and Fee, Gordon D. *Studies in the Theory and Method of New Testament Textual Criticism.* Studies and Documents, no. 45. Grand Rapids: Eerdmans, 1993.

Finegan, Jack. *Encountering New Testament Manuscripts: A Working Introduction to Textual Criticism.* Grand Rapids: Eerdmans, 1974.

Greenlee, J. Harold. *Introduction to New Testament Textual Criticism.* Rev. ed. Peabody, MA: Hendrickson, 1995.

Metzger, Bruce M. *Manuscripts of the Greek Bible: An Introduction to Paleography.* New York: Oxford, 1981.

*———. *The Text of the New Testament: Its Transmission, Corruption, and Restoration.* 3rd ed. Oxford: Oxford University Press, 1992.

*———. *A Textual Commentary on the Greek New Testament.* New York: United Bible Societies, 1971.

*Westcott, Brooke Foss, and Hort, Fenton John Anthony. *Introduction to the New Testament in the Original Greek.* New York: Harper & Row, 1882; reprint, Peabody, MA: Hendrickson, 1988.

Exegetical Method/Hermeneutics

*Black, David Alan, and Dockery, David S. *New Testament Criticism and Interpretation.* Grand Rapids: Zondervan, 1991.

Caird, G. B. *The Language and Imagery of the Bible.* Philadelphia: Westminster, 1980.

*Fee, Gordon D. *New Testament Exegesis: A Handbook for Students and Pastors.* Philadelphia: Westminster, 1983.

Holmberg, Bengt. *Sociology and the New Testament: An Appraisal.* Minneapolis: Fortress, 1990.

Keegan, Terence J. *Interpreting the Bible: A Popular Introduction to Biblical Hermeneutics.* New York: Paulist, 1985.

*Ladd, G. Eldon. *The New Testament and Criticism.* Grand Rapids: Eerdmans, 1967.

Malina, Bruce J. *Christian Origins and Cultural Anthropology: Practical Models for Biblical Interpretation.* Atlanta: John Knox, 1986.

———. *The New Testament World: Insights from Cultural Anthropology.* Atlanta: John Knox, 1981.

*Marshall, I. Howard, ed. *New Testament Interpretation: Essays on Principles and Methods.* Grand Rapids: Eerdmans, 1977.

Osiek, Carolyn. *What are they saying about the Social Setting of the New Testament?* Rev. ed. Paulist: New York, 1992.

Stuhlmacher, Peter. *Historical Criticism and Theological Interpretation of Scripture.* Philadelphia: Fortress, 1977.

*Thiselton, Anthony C. *The Two Horizons: New Testament Hermeneutics and Philosophical Description.* Grand Rapids: Eerdmans, 1980.

Tuckett, Christopher. *Reading the New Testament: Methods of Interpretation.* Philadelphia: Fortress, 1987.

The following volumes in the Guides to Biblical Scholarship series are relevant:

Adam, A. K. M. *What is Postmodern Biblical Criticism?* Minneapolis: Fortress, 1995.

Beardslee, William A. *Literary Criticism of the New Testament.* Philadelphia: Fortress, 1970.

*Elliott, John H. *What is Social-Scientific Criticism?* Minneapolis: Fortress, 1993.

Mack, Burton. *Rhetoric and the New Testament.* Minneapolis: Fortress, 1989.

*McKnight, Edgar V. *What is Form Criticism?* Philadelphia: Fortress, 1969.

Patte, Daniel. *What is Structural Exegesis?* Philadelphia: Fortress, 1976.

———. *Structural Exegesis for New Testament Critics.* Minneapolis: Fortress, 1989.

*Perrin, Norman. *What is Redaction Criticism?* Philadelphia: Fortress, 1969.

*Petersen, Norman R. *Literary Criticism for New Testament Critics.* Philadelphia: Fortress, 1978.

*Powell, Mark Allan. *What is Narrative Criticism?* Minneapolis: Fortress, 1990.

New Testament Surveys

*Barker, Glenn W.; Lane, William L.; and Michaels, J. Ramsey. *The New Testament Speaks.* New York: Harper & Row, 1969.

*Gromacki, Robert G. *New Testament Survey.* Grand Rapids: Eerdmans, 1974.

Marshall, Celia Brewer. *A Guide Through the New Testament.* Louisville: Westminster/John Knox, 1994.

*Metzger, Bruce M. *The New Testament: Its Background, Growth, and Content.* Nashville: Abingdon, 1965.

Tenney, Merrill C. *New Testament Survey.* Rev. ed. Grand Rapids: Eerdmans, 1985.

New Testament Introductions

Carson, D. A.; Moo, Douglas J.; and Morris, Leon. *An Introduction to the New Testament.* Grand Rapids: Zondervan, 1992.

*Childs, Brevard S. *The New Testament as Canon: An Introduction.* Philadelphia: Fortress, 1985.

Fuller, Reginald. *A Critical Introduction to the New Testament.* London: Duckworth, 1966.

*Guthrie, Donald. *New Testament Introduction.* 4th ed. Downers Grove, IL: InterVarsity, 1990.

Koester, Helmut. *Introduction to the New Testament.* 2 vols. Foundations and Facets. Philadelphia: Fortress, 1982.

*Kümmel, Werner Georg. *Introduction to the New Testament.* Rev. ed. Nashville: Abingdon, 1975.

*Martin, Ralph P. *New Testament Foundations.* 2 vols. Grand Rapids: Eerdmans, 1976-1978.

McNeile, Alan Hugh. *An Introduction to the Study of the New Testament.* Rev. ed. Oxford: Clarendon, 1953.

Perrin, Norman, and Duling, Dennis C. *The New Testament: An Introduction.* 2nd ed. New York: Harcourt, Brace, Jovanovich, 1982.

Schweizer, Eduard. *A Theological Introduction to the New Testament.*
Nashville: Abingdon, 1991.

Wikenhauser, Alfred. *New Testament Introduction.* New York: Herder
& Herder, 1958.

New Testament Theology

Bauer, Walter. *Orthodoxy and Heresy in Earliest Christianity.*
Philadelphia: Fortress, 1971.

Boers, Hendrikus. *What is New Testament Theology?* Guides to
Biblical Scholarship. Philadelphia: Fortress, 1979.

Bultmann, Rudolf. *Theology of the New Testament.* Scribner Studies in
Contemporary Theology. New York: Scribner's, 1955.

Caird, G. B. *New Testament Theology.* Edited by L. D. Hurst. Oxford:
Clarendon, 1994.

*Cullmann, Oscar. *Christ and Time: The Primitive Christian Conception
of Time and History.* Rev. ed. Philadelphia: Westminster, 1964.

*———. *The Christology of the New Testament.* Rev. ed. Philadelphia:
Westminster, 1963.

Dodd, C. H. *The Apostolic Preaching and its Developments.* London:
Hodder & Stoughton, 1936.

*Dunn, James D. G. *Unity and Diversity in the New Testament: An
Inquiry into the Character of Earliest Christianity.* Philadelphia:
Westminster, 1977.

*Goppelt, Leonhard. *Theology of the New Testament.* 2 vols. Grand
Rapids: Eerdmans, 1981.

*Guthrie, Donald. *New Testament Theology.* Downers Grove, IL:
InterVarsity, 1981.

Hasel, Gerhard. *New Testament Theology: Basic Issues in the Current
Debate.* Grand Rapids: Eerdmans, 1978.

Hunter, Archibald M. *Introducing New Testament Theology.* Philadelphia: Westminster, 1957.

Jeremias, Joachim. *New Testament Theology.* Volume I. New York: Scribner's, 1971.

Kümmel, Werner Georg. *The Theology of the New Testament according to its Major Witnesses, Jesus—Paul—John.* Nashville: Abingdon, 1973.

*Ladd, George Eldon. *A Theology of the New Testament.* Revised and edited by Donald A. Hagner. Grand Rapids: Eerdmans, 1993.

Richardson, Alan. *An Introduction to the Theology of the New Testament.* London: SCM, 1958.

*Wright, N. T. *The New Testament and the People of God.* Christian Origins and the Question of God, vol. 1. Minneapolis: Fortress, 1992.

New Testament Ethics

Dodd, C. H. *Gospel and Law: The Relation of Faith and Ethics in Early Christianity.* New York: Columbia University Press, 1951.

Furnish, Victor Paul. *The Love Commandment in the New Testament.* Nashville: Abingdon, 1972.

Houlden, J. L. *Ethics and the New Testament.* Harmondsworth, UK: Penguin, 1973.

Lohse, Eduard. *Theological Ethics of the New Testament.* Minneapolis: Fortress, 1991.

Longenecker, Richard. *New Testament Social Ethics for Today.* Grand Rapids, Eerdmans, 1984.

*Marxsen, Willi. *New Testament Foundations for Christian Ethics.* Minneapolis: Fortress, 1989.

*Sanders, Jack T. *Ethics in the New Testament: Change and Development.* London: SCM, 1986.

*Schnackenburg, Rudolf. *The Moral Teaching of the New Testament.* New York: Herder & Herder, 1965.

*Schrage, Wolfgang. *The Ethics of the New Testament.* Minneapolis: Fortress, 1988.

*Verhey, Allen. *The Great Reversal: Ethics and the New Testament.* Grand Rapids: Eerdmans, 1984.

*Yoder, John Howard. *The Politics of Jesus: vicit Agnus noster.* Rev. ed. Grand Rapids: Eerdmans, 1993.

Use of the Old Testament in the New Testament

Bruce, F. F. *New Testament Development of Old Testament Themes.* Grand Rapids: Eerdmans, 1968.

Dodd, C. H. *According to the Scriptures: The Substructure of New Testament Theology.* London: Nisbet, 1952.

*Ellis, E. Earle. *The Old Testament in Early Christianity: Canon and Interpretation in the Light of Modern Research.* Grand Rapids: Baker, 1992.

France, R. T. *Jesus and the Old Testament.* Downers Grove, IL: InterVarsity, 1971.

Goppelt, Leonhard. *Typos: The Typological Interpretation of the Old Testament in the New.* Grand Rapids: Eerdmans, 1981.

*Hayes, Richard B. *Echoes of Scripture in the Letters of Paul.* New Haven, CT: Yale University Press, 1989.

*Juel, Donald. *Messianic Exegesis: Christological Interpretation of the Old Testament in Early Christianity.* Philadelphia: Fortress, 1988.

Lindars, Barnabas. *New Testament Apologetic: The Doctrinal Significance of the Old Testament Quotations.* London: SCM, 1961.

*Longenecker, Richard. *Biblical Exegesis in the Apostolic Period.* Grand Rapids: Eerdmans, 1975.

New Testament Apocrypha

Cameron, Ron, ed. *The Other Gospels: Non-Canonical Gospel Texts.* Philadelphia: Westminster, 1982.

Elliott, J. K., ed. *The Apocryphal New Testament: A Collection of Apocryphal Christian Literature in an English Translation.* Oxford: Oxford University Press, 1994.

*Finegan, Jack. *Hidden Records of the Life of Jesus: An Introduction to the New Testament Apocrypha.* Philadelphia: Pilgrim, 1969.

Grant, Robert M. *The Secret Sayings of Jesus.* Garden City, NJ: Doubleday, 1960.

*Hennecke, Edgar. *New Testament Apocrypha.* Edited by Wilhelm Schneemelcher. 2 vols. Philadelphia: Westminster, 1963.

Pagels, Elaine. *The Gnostic Gospels.* New York: Random House, 1979.

Robinson, J. M., ed. *The Nag Hammadi Library in English.* 3rd. ed. San Francisco: Harper & Row, 1988.

New Testament Commentaries

Alford, Henry. *The Greek New Testament.* 5th ed. 4 vols. London: Rivingtons, 1875; reprint [*Alford's Greek New Testament*], Grand Rapids: Guardian, 1975.

Bengel, John Albert. *Gnomen of the New Testament.* 2 vols. Philadelphia: Perkinpine & Higgins, 1864; reprint [*New Testament Word Studies*], Grand Rapids: Kregel, 1971.

Nicoll, W. Robertson, ed. *The Expositor's Greek Testament.* 5 vols. London: Hodder & Stoughton, 1897-1910; reprint, Grand Rapids: Eerdmans, 1974.

Osborne, Grant R. *The IVP New Testament Commentary Series.* 6 vols. (with more appearing) Downers Grove, IL: InterVarsity, 1992—.

*Wesley, John. *Explanatory Notes upon the New Testament.* London: W. Bowyer, 1755; reprint, London: Epworth, 1950.

Multi-volume commentary series whose individual volumes are frequently listed below under specific biblical books include:

Augsburg Commentary on the New Testament, ed. Roy A. Harrisville; Jack Dean Kingsbury; and Gerhard Krodel (Augsburg/Fortress); *Harper's New Testament Commentaries,* ed. Henry Chadwick (Harper); *New International Commentary on the New Testament,* ed. F. F. Bruce (Eerdmans);*New International Greek Testament Commentary,* ed. I. Howard Marshall and W. Ward Gasque (Eerdmans); *Proclamation Commentaries: The New Testament Witnesses for Preaching,* ed. Gerhard Krodel (Fortress); *Tyndale New Testament Commentaries,* ed. R. V. G. Tasker (Eerdmans). With this kind of multi-volume commentaries, it is generally advisable to select individual volumes rather than purchase the whole set; individual volumes tend to vary in terms of quality and usefulness.

The Gospels: General Works

Studies in the Gospels Themselves:

*Brown, Raymond E. *The Birth of the Messiah: A Commentary on the Infancy Narratives in the Gospels of Matthew and Luke.* Rev. ed. Anchor Bible Reference Library. New York: Doubleday, 1993.

*———. *The Death of the Messiah: A Commentary on the Passion Narratives.* 2 vols. Anchor Bible Reference Library. New York: Doubleday, 1994.

Bultmann, Rudolf. *The History of the Synoptic Tradition.* Rev. ed. New York: Harper & Row, 1963.

Catchpole, David. *The Quest for Q.* Edinburgh: T. & T. Clark, 1994.

Dibelius, Martin. *From Tradition to Gospel.* Cambridge: James Clarke, 1971.

Farmer, William Reuben. *The Synoptic Problem: A Critical Analysis.* New York: Macmillan, 1964.

*Green, Joel B.; McKnight, Scot; and Marshall, I. Howard. *Dictionary of Jesus and the Gospels: A Compendium of Contemporary Biblical Scholarship.* Downers Grove, IL: InterVarsity, 1992.

Hastings, James, ed. *A Dictionary of Christ and the Gospels.* 2 vols. Edinburgh: T. & T. Clark, 1906.

*Kingsbury, Jack Dean. *Jesus Christ in Matthew, Mark, and Luke.* Proclamation Commentaries. Philadelphia: Fortress, 1981.

Lightfoot, Robert Henry. *History and Interpretation in the Gospels.* London: Hodder and Stoughton, 1935.

Manson, T. W. *The Sayings of Jesus: As Recorded in the Gospels according to St. Matthew and St. Luke arranged with Introduction and Commentary.* London: SCM, 1949; reprint, Grand Rapids: Eerdmans, 1979

*Mays, James Luther, ed. *Interpreting the Gospels.* Philadelphia: Fortress, 1981.

*Rohde, Joachim. *Rediscovering the Teaching of the Evangelists.* New Testament Library. London: SCM, 1968.

Stonehouse, Ned B. *The Witness of the Synoptic Gospels to Christ.* Grand Rapids: Baker, 1979. Reprint of *The Witness of Matthew and Mark to Christ* (Philadelphia: Presbyterian Guardian, 1944); and *The Witness of Luke to Christ* (Grand Rapids: Eerdmans, 1951).

*Streeter, Burnett Hillman. *The Four Gospels: A Study in Origins.* London: Macmillan, 1926.

Talbert, Charles H. *What is a Gospel? The Genre of the Canonical Gospels.* Philadelphia: Fortress, 1977.

Taylor, Vincent. *The Formation of the Gospel Tradition.* London: Macmillan, 1960.

Theissen, Gerd. *The Gospels in Context: Social and Political History in the Synoptic Tradition.* Minneapolis: Fortress, 1991.

———. *The Miracle Stories of the Early Christian Tradition.* Philadelphia: Fortress, 1983.

Studies in the Life of Christ:

Borg, Marcus J. *Jesus: A New Vision.* San Francisco: Harper & Row, 1987.

Bornkamm, Günther. *Jesus of Nazareth.* New York: Harper & Brothers, 1960.

Conzelmann, Hans. *Jesus.* Philadelphia: Fortress, 1973.

Crossan, John Dominic. *The Historical Jesus: The Life of a Mediterranean Jewish Peasant.* San Francisco: Harper, 1991.

Dalman, Gustaf. *The Words of Jesus: Considered in the Light of Post-Biblical Jewish Writings and the Aramaic Language.* Edinburgh: T. & T. Clark, 1902; reprint, Minneapolis: Klock & Klock, 1981.

Dodd, C. H. *The Founder of Christianity.* New York: Macmillan, 1970.

Dunn, James D. G. *The Evidence for Jesus.* Atlanta: John Knox, 1985.

Evans, Craig. A. *Jesus.* IBR Bibliographies, no. 5. Grand Rapids: Baker, 1992.

*Guthrie, Donald. *Jesus the Messiah: An Illustrated Life of Christ.* Grand Rapids: Zondervan, 1972.

———. *A Shorter Life of Christ.* Grand Rapids: Zondervan, 1970.

*Kähler, Martin. *The So-Called Historical Jesus and the Historic Biblical Christ.* Philadelphia: Fortress, 1964. (Originally published, in German, in 1896.)

Mack, Burton L. *A Myth of Innocence: Mark and Christian Origins.* Philadelphia: Fortress, 1988.

*Marshall, I. Howard. *I Believe in the Historical Jesus.* Grand Rapids: Eerdmans, 1977.

*Meier, John P. *A Marginal Jew: Rethinking the Historical Jesus.* 3 vols. Anchor Bible Reference Library. New York: Doubleday, 1991, 1994. (Volumes 1 and 2 presently available.)

*O'Collins, Gerald. *What are they Saying about Jesus?* Rev. ed. New York: Paulist, 1983.

Robinson, James M. *A New Quest of the Historical Jesus.* Studies in Biblical Theology, no. 25. London: SCM, 1959.

*Sanders, E. P. *Jesus and Judaism.* Philadelphia: Fortress, 1985.

———. *The Historical Figure of Jesus.* New York: Penguin, 1994.

*Schweitzer, Albert. *The Quest of the Historical Jesus: A Critical Study of its Progress from Reimarus to Wrede.* New York: Macmillan, 1968. (Originally published, in German, in 1906.)

Strauss, David Friedrich. *The Life of Jesus Critically Examined.* Lives of Jesus Series. Philadelphia: Fortress, 1972. (Originally published, in German, in 1835.)

Stuhlmacher, Peter. *Jesus of Nazareth, Christ of Faith.* Peabody, MA: Hendrickson, 1993.

Vermes, Geza. *Jesus the Jew: A Historian's Reading of the Gospels.* London: Collins, 1973.

———. *The Religion of Jesus the Jew.* Minneapolis: Fortress, 1993.

*Weiss, Johannes. *Jesus' Proclamation of the Kingdom of God.* Philadelphia: Fortress, 1971.

*Witherington III, Ben C. *The Christology of Jesus.* Minneapolis: Fortress, 1990.

*———. *Jesus the Sage: The Pilgrimage of Wisdom.* Minneapolis: Fortress, 1994.

*Witherington III, Ben C. *The Jesus Quest: The Third Search for the Jew of Nazareth.* Downers Grove, IL: InterVarsity, 1995.

*Wright, N. T. *Who Was Jesus?* Grand Rapids: Eerdmans, 1992.

Studies in the Parables:

Bailey, Kenneth E. *Through Peasant Eyes: More Lucan Parables, Their Culture and Style.* Grand Rapids: Eerdmans, 1980.

Blomberg, Craig L. *Interpreting the Parables.* Downers Grove, IL: InterVarsity, 1990.

Borsch, Frederick Houk. *Many Things in Parables: Extravagant Stories of New Community.* Philadelphia: Fortress, 1988.

*Dodd, C. H. *The Parables of the Kingdom.* New York: Scribner's, 1961.

Donahue, John R. *The Gospel in Parable: Metaphor, Narrative and Theology in the Synoptic Gospels.* Philadelphia: Fortress, 1988.

*Jeremias, Joachim. *Rediscovering the Parables.* New York: Scribner's, 1966.

*Kingsbury, Jack Dean. *The Parables of Jesus in Matthew 13: A Study in Redaction Criticism.* London: SCM, 1969.

Lambrecht, Jan. *Out of the Treasure: The Parables in the Gospel of Matthew.* Louvain Theological & Pastoral Monographs, no. 10. Louvain: Peeters, 1991.

*Scott, Bernard Brandon. *Hear Then the Parable: A Commentary on the Parables of Jesus.* Minneapolis: Fortress, 1989.

Stein, Robert H. *An Introduction to the Parables of Jesus.* Philadelphia: Westminster/John Knox, 1981.

*Tolbert, Mary Ann. *Perspectives on the Parables: An Approach to Multiple Interpretations.* Philadelphia: Fortress, 1979.

Westermann, Claus. *The Parables of Jesus in Light of the Old Testament.* Edinburgh: T. & T. Clark, 1990.

Gospel Harmonies/Synopses

*Aland, Kurt, ed. *Synopsis Quattuor Evangeliorum.* 9th rev. ed. Stuttgart: Deutsche Bibelstiftung, 1976.

Funk, Robert W. *New Gospel Parallels: John and the Other Gospels.* Sonoma, CA: Polebridge, 1985.

———. *New Gospel Parallels: Vol. 1,2—Mark.* Sonoma, CA: Polebridge, 1990.

Huck, Albert. *A Synopsis of the First Three Gospels with the Addition of the Johannine Parallels.* Grand Rapids: Eerdmans, 1982.

Stevens, William Arnold, and Burton, Ernest De Witt. *A Harmony of the Gospels for Historical Study.* New York: Scribner's, 1932.

*Throckmorton, Burton H. *Gospel Parallels: A Comparison of the Synoptic Gospels.* 5th ed. Nashville: Nelson, 1992.

Matthew

Bauer, David R. *The Structure of Matthew's Gospel: A Study in Literary Design.* Journal for the Study of the New Testament Supplement Series, no. 31. Sheffield: Almond, 1988.

Beare, Francis Wright. *The Gospel according to Matthew.* San Francisco: Harper & Row, 1981.

Bornkamm, Günther; Barth, Gerhard; and Held, Heinz Joachim. *Tradition and Interpretation in Matthew.* New Testament Library. Philadelphia: Westminster, 1963.

*Davies, William David; and Allison, Dale C. *A Critical and Exegetical Commentary on the Gospel according to Saint Matthew.* 3 vols. International Critical Commentary. Edinburgh: T. & T. Clark, 1988, 1991. (Volumes I and II are currently available.)

*France, R. T. *Matthew: Evangelist and Teacher.* Grand Rapids: Zondervan, 1989.

Garland, David E. *Reading Matthew: A Literary and Theological Commentary on the First Gospel.* New York: Crossroad, 1993.

Gundry, Robert H. *Matthew: A Commentary on His Handbook for a Mixed Church under Persecution.* Grand Rapids: Eerdmans, 1994.

*Hagner, Donald A. *Matthew 1-13.* Word Biblical Commentary. Dallas: Word, 1993.

Hare, Douglas R. A. *Matthew.* Interpretation: A Bible Commentary for Teaching and Preaching. Louisville: Westminster/John Knox, 1993.

Harrington, Daniel J. *The Gospel of Matthew.* Sacra Pagina. Collegeville, MN: Michael Glazier, 1991.

*Hill, David. *The Gospel of Matthew.* New Century Bible Commentary. Grand Rapids: Eerdmans, 1972.

*Kingsbury, Jack Dean. *Matthew.* 2nd ed. Proclamation Commentaries. Philadelphia: Fortress, 1986.

*———. *Matthew as Story.* Rev. ed. Philadelphia: Fortress, 1988.

*———. *Matthew: Structure, Christology, Kingdom.* With a new preface. Minneapolis: Fortress, 1989.

Luz, Ulrich. *Matthew 1-7: A Commentary.* Minneapolis: Augsburg, 1989. (Volume I of three-volume work is currently available)

McNeile, Alan Hugh. *The Gospel according to St. Matthew: The Greek Text with Introduction, Notes, and Indices.* London: Macmillan, 1938.

Meier, John P. *The Vision of Matthew: Christ, Church, and Morality in the First Gospel.* New York: Paulist, 1979.

Plummer, Alfred. *An Exegetical Commentary on the Gospel according to Matthew.* London: Robert Scott, 1909.

Schweizer, Eduard. *The Good News according to Matthew.* Atlanta: John Knox, 1975.

Senior, Donald. *What are they Saying about Matthew?* New York: Paulist, 1983.

Stanton, Graham, ed. *The Interpretation of Matthew.* Rev. ed. Issues in Religion and Theology, no. 3. Philadelphia: Fortress, 1994.

Studies on the Sermon on the Mount include the following:

*Betz, Hans Dieter. *The Sermon on the Mount: A Commentary on the Sermon on the Mount, Including the Sermon on the Plain (Matthew 5:3-7:27 and Luke 6:20-49).* Hermeneia: A Critical and Historical Commentary on the Bible. Minneapolis: Fortress, 1995.

Carter, Warren. *What are they saying about Matthew's Sermon on the Mount?* New York: Paulist, 1994.

*Davies, William David. *The Setting of the Sermon on the Mount.* Cambridge: Cambridge University Press, 1966.

*Guelich, Robert A. *The Sermon on the Mount: A Foundation for Understanding.* Waco, TX: Word, 1982.

Strecker, Georg. *The Sermon on the Mount: An Exegetical Commentary.* Nashville: Abingdon, 1988.

Mark

Achtemeier, Paul J. *Mark.* 2nd ed. Proclamation Commentaries. Philadelphia: Fortress, 1986.

*Anderson, Hugh. *The Gospel of Mark.* New Century Bible Commentary. Grand Rapids: Eerdmans, 1976.

Anderson, Janice Capel, and Moore, Stephen D. *Mark and Method: New Approaches in Biblical Studies.* Minneapolis: Fortress, 1992.

Best, Ernest. *Mark: The Gospel as Story.* Edinburgh: T. & T. Clark, 1983.

*Cranfield, C. E. B. *The Gospel according to St. Mark.* Cambridge Greek Testament Commentary. Cambridge: Cambridge University Press, 1977.

*Guelich, Robert A. *Mark 1-8:26.* Word Biblical Commentary. Waco, TX: Word, 1989.

*Gundry, Robert H. *Mark: A Commentary on His Apology for the Cross.* Grand Rapids: Eerdmans, 1993.

Hengel, Martin. *Studies in the Gospel of Mark.* Philadelphia: Fortress, 1985.

*Hooker, Morna D. *The Gospel according to St. Mark.* Black's New Testament Commentary. Peabody, MA: Hendrickson, 1991.

Juel, Donald. *A Master of Surprise: Mark Interpreted.* Minneapolis: Fortress, 1994.

*Kealy, Seán P. *Mark's Gospel: A History of its Interpretation: From the Beginning Until 1979.* New York: Paulist, 1982.

*Kingsbury, Jack Dean. *The Christology of Mark's Gospel.* Philadelphia: Fortress, 1983.

*———. *Conflict in Mark: Jesus, Authorities, Disciples.* Philadelphia: Fortress, 1989.

*Lane, William L. *Commentary on the Gospel of Mark.* New International Commentary on the New Testament. Grand Rapids: Eerdmans, 1974.

Lightfoot, Robert Henry. *The Gospel Message of St. Mark.* Oxford: Clarendon, 1950.

*Martin, Ralph. *Mark: Evangelist and Theologian.* Contemporary Evangelical Perspectives. Grand Rapids: Zondervan, 1973.

Matera, Frank. *What are they Saying about Mark?* New York: Paulist, 1987.

*Rhoades, David, and Michie, Donald. *Mark as Story: An Introduction to the Narrative of a Gospel.* Philadelphia: Fortress, 1982.

*Robbins, Vernon K. *Jesus the Teacher: A Socio-Rhetorical Interpretation of Mark.* With a new introduction. Minneapolis: Fortress, 1992.

Schweizer, Eduard. *The Good News according to Mark.* Atlanta: John Knox, 1970.

Taylor, Vincent. *The Gospel according to St. Mark: The Greek Text with Introduction, Notes, and Indexes.* London: Macmillan, 1952.

Telford, William. R., ed. *The Interpretation of Mark.* Rev. ed. Edinburgh: T. & T. Clark, 1994.

*Tolbert, Mary Ann. *Sowing the Gospel: Mark's World in Literary-Historical Perspective.* Minneapolis: Fortress, 1989.

Tuckett, Christopher. *The Messianic Secret.* Issues in Religion and Theology, no. 1. Philadelphia: Fortress, 1983.

Weeden, Theodore J., Jr. *Mark: Traditions in Conflict.* Philadelphia: Fortress, 1971.

Williamson, Lamar, Jr. *Mark.* Interpretation: A Bible Commentary for Teaching and Preaching. Atlanta: John Knox, 1983.

Wrede, William. *The Messianic Secret.* Library of Theological Translations. Cambridge: James Clarke, 1971. (Originally published, in German, in 1901)

Luke and Luke-Acts (See also under Acts)

Brawley, Robert L. *Centering on God: Method and Message in Luke-Acts.* Literary Currents in Biblical Interpretation. Louisville: Westminster/John Knox, 1990.

Conzelmann, Hans. *The Theology of St. Luke.* New York: Harper & Row, 1960; reprint, Philadelphia: Fortress, 1982.

Craddock, Fred B. *Luke.* Interpretation: A Bible Commentary for Teaching and Preaching. Louisville, John Knox, 1990.

*Darr, John A. *On Character Building: The Reader and the Rhetoric of Characterization in Luke-Acts.* Literary Currents in Biblical Interpretation. Louisville: Westminster/John Knox, 1992.

Ellis, E. Earle. *The Gospel of Luke.* Rev. ed. New Century Bible Commentary. Grand Rapids: Eerdmans, 1974.

*Fitzmyer, Joseph A. *The Gospel according to Luke.* 2 vols. Anchor Bible. Garden City, NY: Doubleday, 1981, 1985.

———. *Luke the Theologian: Aspects of His Teaching.* New York: Paulist, 1989.

*Franklin, Eric. *Christ the Lord: A Study in the Purpose and Theology of Luke-Acts.* Philadelphia: Westminster, 1975.

Green, Joel B., and McKeever, Michael C. *Luke-Acts and New Testament Historiography.* IBR Bibliographies, no. 8. Grand Rapids: Baker, 1994.

*Johnson, Luke Timothy. *The Gospel of Luke.* Sacra Pagina. Collegeville, MN: Michael Glazier, 1991.

*Kingsbury, Jack Dean. *Conflict in Luke.* Minneapolis: Fortress, 1991.

Kurz, William S. *Reading Luke-Acts: Dynamics of Biblical Narrative.* Louisville: Westminster/John Knox, 1993.

Maddox, Robert. *The Purpose of Luke-Acts.* Studies of the New Testament and its World. Edinburgh: T. & T. Clark, 1982.

*Marshall, I. Howard. *The Gospel of Luke: A Commentary on the Greek Text.* New International Greek Testament Commentary. Grand Rapids: Eerdmans, 1978.

*———. *Luke: Historian and Theologian.* Contemporary Evangelical Perspectives. Grand Rapids: Zondervan, 1970.

Neyrey, Jerome H., ed. *The Social World of Luke-Acts: Models for Interpretation.* Peabody, MA: Hendrickson, 1991.

Nolland, John. *Luke 1-9:20.* Word Biblical Commentary. Waco, TX: Word, 1989.

——. *Luke 9:21-18:34.* Word Biblical Commentary. Dallas: Word, 1993.

——. *Luke 18:35-24:53.* Word Biblical Commentary. Dallas: Word, 1993.

Plummer, Alfred. *A Critical and Exegetical Commentary on the Gospel according to S. Luke.* International Critical Commentary. Edinburgh: T. & T. Clark, 1910.

Powell, Mark Allan. *What are they saying about Luke?* New York: Paulist, 1989.

Schweizer, Eduard. *The Good News according to Luke.* Atlanta: John Knox, 1984.

*Talbert, Charles H. *Reading Luke: A Literary and Theological Commentary on the Third Gospel.* New York: Crossroad, 1982.

Tannehill, Robert. *The Narrative Unity of Luke-Acts: A Literary Interpretation. Volume One: The Gospel according to Luke.* Foundations & Facets: New Testament. Philadelphia: Fortress, 1986.

Tyson, Joseph B. *Luke-Acts and the Jewish People: Eight Critical Perspectives.* Minneapolis: Augsburg, 1988.

John and the Johannine School (See also under Epistles of John)

Ashton, John. *The Interpretation of John.* Issues in Religion and Theology, no. 9. Philadelphia: Fortress, 1986.

*Barrett, C. K. *The Gospel according to St. John: An Introduction with Commentary and Notes on the Greek Text.* 2nd ed. Philadelphia: Westminster, 1978.

*Barrett, C. K. *Essays on John*. Philadelphia: Westminster, 1982.

*Beasley-Murray, George R. *John*. Word Biblical Commentary. Waco, TX: Word, 1987.

Bernard, J. H. *A Critical and Exegetical Commentary on the Gospel according to St. John*. 2 vols. International Critical Commentary. Edinburgh: T. & T. Clark, 1928.

*Brown, Raymond E. *The Gospel according to John*. 2 vols. Anchor Bible. Garden City, NY: Doubleday, 1966, 1970.

———. *The Community of the Beloved Disciple: The Life, Loves, and Hates of an Individual Church in New Testament Times*. New York: Paulist, 1979

*Bruce, F. F. *The Gospel of John*. Grand Rapids: Eerdmans, 1983.

Cullmann, Oscar. *The Johannine Circle*. Philadelphia: Westminster, 1976.

*Culpepper, R. Alan. *Anatomy of the Fourth Gospel: A Study in Literary Design*. Foundations & Facets: New Testament. Philadelphia: Fortress, 1983.

Dodd, C. H. *The Interpretation of the Fourth Gospel*. Cambridge: Cambridge University Press, 1954.

Haenchen, Ernst. *John*. 2 vols. Hermeneia: A Critical and Historical Commentary on the Bible. Philadelphia: Fortress, 1984.

*Hengel, Martin. *The Johannine Question*. Philadelphia: Trinity Press International, 1989.

*Hoskyns, Edwyn. *The Fourth Gospel*. Edited by Francis Noel Davey. Rev. ed. London: Faber & Faber, 1947.

*Morris, Leon. *The Gospel according to John*. New International Commentary on the New Testament. Rev. ed. Grand Rapids: Eerdmans, 1995.

———. *Studies in the Fourth Gospel*. Grand Rapids: Eerdmans, 1967.

*Schnackenburg, Rudolf. *The Gospel according to St. John.* 3 vols. New York: Crossroad, 1987.

Sloyan, Gerard. *John.* Interpretation: A Bible Commentary for Teaching and Preaching. Atlanta: John Knox, 1988.

*———. *What are they saying about John?* New York: Paulist, 1991.

*Smalley, Stephen S. *John: Evangelist and Interpreter.* London: Paternoster, 1978; reprint, Nashville: Thomas Nelson, 1983.

Smith, D. Moody. *John Among the Gospels: The Relationship in Twentieth-Century Research.* Minneapolis: Fortress, 1992.

*———. *The Theology of the Gospel of John.* New Testament Theology. Cambridge: Cambridge University Press, 1995.

Talbert, Charles H. *Reading John: A Literary and Theological Commentary on the Fourth Gospel and the Johannine Epistles.* New York: Crossroad, 1992.

Turner, George Allen, and Mantey, Julius R. *The Gospel of John.* Evangelical Commentary on the Bible. Grand Rapids: Eerdmans, 1964.

Westcott, Brooke Foss. *The Gospel according to John.* The Speakers Bible. London: John Murray, 1881; reprint, Grand Rapids: Eerdmans, 1967.

Acts of the Apostles

*Barrett, C. K. *A Critical and Exegetical Commentary on the Acts of the Apostles.* 2 vols. International Critical Commentary. Edinburgh: T. & T. Clark, 1994. (Volume I is presently available.)

*Bauckham, Richard. *The Book of Acts in its Palestinian Setting.* The Book of Acts in its First Century Setting, vol. 4. Grand Rapids: Eerdmans, 1995.

*Bruce, F. F. *Commentary on the Book of Acts.* Rev. ed. New International Commentary on the New Testament. Grand Rapids: Eerdmans, 1988.

Carter, Charles; and Earle, Ralph. *The Acts of the Apostles.* Zondervan Commentaries. Grand Rapids: Zondervan, 1973.

Conzelmann, Hans. *Acts of the Apostles.* Heremeneia: A Critical and Historical Commentary on the Bible. Philadelphia: Fortress, 1987.

Foakes-Jackson, F. J., and Lake, Kirsopp, eds. *The Acts of the Apostles.* 5 vols. London: Macmillan, 1920-1933.

Gasque, W. Ward. *A History of the Criticism of the Acts of the Apostles.* Rev. ed. Peabody, MA: Hendrickson, 1989.

*Gill, David W. J., and Gempf, Conrad, eds. *The Book of Acts in its Graeco-Roman Setting.* The Book of Acts in its First Century Setting, vol. 2. Grand Rapids: Eerdmans, 1994.

Haenchen, Ernst. *The Acts of the Apostles: A Commentary.* Philadelphia: Westminster, 1971.

Hemer, Colin J. *The Book of Acts in the Setting of Hellenistic History.* Winona Lake, IN: Eisenbrauns, 1990.

Hengel, Martin. *Acts and the History of Earliest Christianity.* Philadelphia: Fortress, 1980.

*Johnson, Luke Timothy. *The Acts of the Apostles.* Sacra Pagina. Collegeville, MN: Michael Glazier, 1992.

*Kee, Howard Clark. *Good News to the Ends of the Earth: The Theology of Acts.* Philadelphia: Trinity Press International, 1990.

*Marshall, I. Howard. *The Acts of the Apostles.* Tyndale New Testament Commentaries. Grand Rapids: Eerdmans, 1980.

Munck, Johannes. *The Acts of the Apostles.* Anchor Bible. New York: Doubleday, 1967.

*Powell, Mark Allan. *What are they saying about Acts?* New York: Paulist, 1991.

Rackham, Richard Belward. *The Acts of the Apostles: An Exposition.* 14th ed. Westminster Commentaries. London: Methuen, 1901; reprint, Grand Rapids: Baker, 1978.

*Rapske, Brian. *The Book of Acts and Paul in Roman Custody.* The Book of Acts in its First Century Setting, vol. 3. Grand Rapids: Eerdmans, 1994.

Soards, Marion L. *The Speeches in Acts: Their Content, Context, and Concerns.* Louisville: Westminster/John Knox, 1994.

Tannehill, Robert. *The Narrative Unity of Luke-Acts: A Literary Interpretation. Volume Two: The Acts of the Apostles.* Foundations & Facets: New Testament. Minneapolis: Fortress, 1986.

*Willimon, William. *Acts.* Interpretation: A Bible Commentary for Teaching and Preaching. Atlanta: John Knox, 1988.

*Winter, Bruce W., and Clarke, Andrew D., eds. *The Book of Acts in its Ancient Literary Setting.* The Book of Acts in its First Century Setting, vol. 1. Grand Rapids: Eerdmans, 1993.

New Testament Epistles

*Doty, W. G. *Letters in Primitive Christianity.* Guides to Biblical Scholarship. Philadelphia: Fortress, 1973.

*Malherbe, Abraham. *Moral Exhortation: A Greco-Roman Sourcebook.* Library of Early Christianity. Philadelphia: Westminster, 1986.

Stirewalt, M. Luther, Jr. *Studies in Ancient Greek Epistolography.* Atlanta: Scholars, 1993.

Stowers, Stanley K. *Letter Writing in Greco-Roman Antiquity.* Library of Early Christianity. Philadelphia: Westminster, 1986.

Paul

*Barrett, C. K. *Essays on Paul.* Philadelphia: Westminster, 1982.

*Barrett, C. K. *From First Adam to Last: A Fresh Approach to Some Problems of Paul and the New Testament.* New York: Scribner's, 1962.

*———. *Paul: An Introduction to His Thought.* Louisville: Westminster/John Knox, 1994.

*Bassler, Jouette M., ed. *Pauline Theology, Volume I: Thessalonians, Philippians, Galatians, Philemon.* Minneapolis: Fortress, 1991.

*Becker, Jürgen. *Paul: Apostle to the Gentiles.* Louisville: Westminster/John Knox, 1993.

*Beker, J. Christiaan. *Paul the Apostle: The Triumph of God in Life and Thought.* Philadelphia: Fortress, 1980.

Bornkamm, Günther. *Paul.* New York: Harper & Row, 1971.

*Bruce, F. F. *Paul: Apostle of the Heart Set Free.* Grand Rapids: Eerdmans, 1977.

Davies, W. D. *Paul and Rabbinic Judaism: Some Rabbinic Elements in Pauline Theology.* London: SPCK, 1948.

*Donfried, Karl P., and Marshall, I. Howard. *The Theology of the Shorter Pauline Letters.* New Testament Theology. Cambridge: Cambridge University Press, 1993.

*Fee, Gordon D. *God's Empowering Presence: The Holy Spirit in the Letters of Paul.* Peabody, MA: Hendrickson, 1994.

*Hawthorne, Gerald F.; Martin, Ralph P.; and Reid, Daniel G., eds. *Dictionary of Paul and His Letters: A Compendium of Contemporary Biblical Scholarship.* Downers Grove, IL: InterVarsity, 1993.

Hübner, Hans. *Law in Paul's Thought.* Studies of the New Testament and its World. Edinburgh: T. & T. Clark, 1984.

Jewett, Robert. *Paul the Apostle to America: Current Trends and Pauline Scholarship.* Louisville: Westminster/John Knox, 1994.

Keck, Leander. *Paul and His Letters.* Rev. ed. Proclamation Commentaries. Philadelphia: Fortress, 1988.

*Longenecker, Richard. *The Ministry and Message of Paul.* Grand
Rapids: Zondervan, 1971.

Meeks, Wayne. *The First Urban Christians: The Social World of the
Apostle Paul.* New Haven, CT: Yale University Press, 1983.

Munck, Johannes. *Paul and the Salvation of Mankind.* Atlanta: John
Knox, 1959.

Neyrey, Jerome. *Paul, In Other Words: A Cultural Reading of His
Letters.* Louisville: Westminster/John Knox, 1990.

Plevnik, Joseph. *What are they saying about Paul?* New York: Paulist,
1986.

Räisänen, Heikki. *Paul & the Law.* Philadelphia: Fortress, 1983.

*Ridderbos, Herman. *Paul: An Outline of His Theology.* Grand Rapids:
Eerdmans, 1975.

*Sanders, E. P. *Paul and Rabbinic Judaism: A Comparison of Patterns of
Religion.* Philadelphia: Fortress, 1977.

*Stewart, James S. *A Man in Christ: The Vital Elements of St. Paul's
Religion.* Grand Rapids: Baker, 1975.

*Witherington III, Ben C. *Paul's Narrative Thought World: The Tapestry
of Tragedy and Triumph.* Louisville: Westminster/John Knox, 1994.

*———. *Jesus, Paul, and the End of the World: A Comparative Study in
New Testament Eschatology.* Downers Grove, IL: InterVarsity, 1992.

*Wright, N. T. *The Climax of the Covenant: Christ and the Law in Pauline
Theology.* Minneapolis: Fortress, 1993.

Romans

*Achtemeier, Paul J. *Romans.* Interpretation: A Bible Commentary for
Teaching and Preaching. Atlanta: John Knox, 1985.

*Barrett, C. K. *The Epistle to the Romans.* Rev. ed. Black's New Testament Commentaries. Peabody, MA: Hendricson, 1991.

Barth, Karl. *The Epistle to the Romans.* London: Oxford, 1933.

Boers, Hendrikus. *The Justification of the Gentiles: Paul's Letters to the Romans and Galatians.* Peabody, MA: Hendrickson, 1994.

Bruce, F. F. *The Epistle to the Romans.* Tyndale New Testament Commentarieds. Grand Rapids: Eerdmans, 1963.

*Cranfield, C. E. B. *A Critical and Exegetical Commentary on the Epistle to the Romans.* 2 vols. International Critical Commentary. Edinburgh: T. & T. Clark, 1975, 1979.

*Donfried, Karl P. *The Romans Debate.* Rev. ed. Peabody, MA: Hendrickson, 1991.

*Dunn, James D. G. *Romans 1-8.* Word Biblical Commentary. Dallas: Word, 1988.

*———. *Romans 9-16.* Word Biblical Commentary. Dallas: Word, 1988.

*Fitzmyer, Joseph A. *Romans.* Anchor Bible. New York: Doubleday, 1993.

*Käsemann, Ernst. *Commentary on Romans.* Grand Rapids: Eerdmans, 1980.

Nygren, Anders. *Commentary on Romans.* Philadelphia: Muhlenberg, 1949.

*Sanday, William, and Headlam, Arthur. *A Critical and Exegetical Commentary on the Epistle to the Romans.* International Critical Commentary. Edinburgh: T. & T. Clark, 1898.

*Schlatter, Adolf. *Romans: The Righteousness of God.* Peabody, MA: Hendrickson, 1995. (Originally published, in German, in 1935.)

Stendahl, Krister. *Final Account: Paul's Letter to the Romans.* Minneapolis: Fortress, 1995.

*Stuhlmacher, Peter. *Paul's Letter to the Romans: A Commentary.* Louisville: Westminster/John Knox, 1994.

Wedderburn, A. J. M. *The Reasons for Romans.* Edinburgh: T. & T. Clark, 1991.

Corinthian Epistles

*Barrett, C. K. *The First Epistle to the Corinthians.* Harper's New Testament Commentaries. New York: Harper & Row, 1968.

*———. *The Second Epistle to the Corinthians.* Harper's New Testament Commentaries. New York: Harper & Row, 1973.

Best, Ernest. *Second Corinthians.* Interpretation: A Bible Commentary for Teaching and Preaching. Atlanta: John Knox, 1987.

*Conzelmann, Hans. *1 Corinthians.* Hermeneia: A Critical and Historical Commentary on the Bible. Philadelphia: Fortress, 1975.

*Fee, Gordon D. *The First Epistle to the Corinthians.* New International Commentary on the New Testament. Grand Rapids: Eerdmans, 1987.

*Furnish, Victor Paul. *2 Corinthians.* Anchor Bible. Garden City, NY: Doubleday, 1984.

Grosheide, F. W. *Commentary on the First Epistle to the Corinthians.* New International Commentary on the New Testament. Grand Rapids: Eerdmans, 1953.

*Hay, David M. *Pauline Theology, Volume II: 1 & 2 Corinthians.* Minneapolis: Fortress, 1993.

*Hering, Jean. *The Second Epistle of St. Paul to the Corinthians.* London: Epworth, 1967.

Hughes, Philip E. *Commentary on the Second Epistle to the Corinthians.* New International Commentary on the New Testament. Grand Rapids: Eerdmans, 1962.

*Martin, Ralph P. *2 Corinthians*. Word Biblical Commentary. Waco, TX: Word, 1986.

Mitchell, Margaret M. *Paul and the Rhetoric of Reconciliation: An Exegetical Investigation of the Language and Composition of 1 Corinthians*. Louisville: Westminster/John Knox, 1991.

*Murphy-O'Connor, Jerome. *The Theology of the Second Letter to the Corinthians*. New Testament Theology. Cambridge: Cambridge University Press, 1991.

Plummer, Alfred. *A Critical and Exegetical Commentary on the Second Epistle of St. Paul to the Corinthians*. International Critical Commentary. Edinburgh: T. & T. Clark, 1915.

Robertson, Archibald, and Plummer, Alfred. *A Critical and Exegetical Commentary on the First Epistle of St. Paul to the Corinthians*. International Critical Commentary. Edinburgh: T. & T. Clark, 1911.

*Talbert, Charles H. *Reading Corinthians: A Literary and Theological Commentary on 1 and 2 Corinthians*. New York: Crossroads, 1987.

Theissen, Gerd. *The Social Setting of Pauline Christianity: Essays on Corinth*. Philadelphia: Fortress, 1982.

*Thrall, Margaret E. *A Critical and Exegetical Commentary on the Second Epistle to the Corinthians*. 2 vols. International Critical Commentary. Edinburgh: T. & T. Clark, 1994. (Volume I is presently available.)

*———. *The First and Second Letters of Paul to the Corinthians*. Cambridge Bible Commentary. Cambridge: Cambridge University Press, 1965.

*Witherington III, Ben C. *Conflict & Community in Corinth: A Socio-Rhetorical Commentary on 1 and 2 Corinthians*. Grand Rapids: Eerdmans, 1995.

Galatians

Barclay, John M. G. *Obeying the Truth: Paul's Ethics in Galatians.* Minneapolis: Fortress, 1991.

*Barrett, C. K. *Freedom and Obligation: A Study of the Epistle to the Galatians.* Philadelphia: Westminster, 1985.

*Betz, Hans Dieter. *Galatians.* Hermeneia: A Critical and Historical Commentary on the Bible. Philadelphia: Fortress, 1979.

*Bruce, F. F. *The Epistle to the Galatians: A Commentary on the Greek Text.* New International Greek Testament Commentary. Grand Rapids: Eerdmans, 1982.

Burton, Ernest De Witt. *A Critical and Exegetical Commentary on the Epistle to the Galatians.* International Critical Commentary. Edinburgh: T. & T. Clark, 1921.

Cousar, Charles B. *Galatians.* Interpretation: A Bible Commentary for Teaching and Preaching. Atlanta: John Knox, 1982.

*Dunn, James D. G. *The Epistle to the Galatians.* Black's New Testament Commentaries. Peabody, MA: Hendrickson, 1993.

*——. *The Theology of Paul's Letter to the Galatians.* New Testament Theology. Cambridge: Cambridge University Press, 1993.

*Fung, Ronald Y. K. *The Epistle to the Galatians.* New International Commentary on the New Testament. Grand Rapids: Eerdmans, 1988.

*Lightfoot, Joseph Barber. *The Epistle of St. Paul to the Galatians.* London: Macmillan, 1865; reprint [Zondervan Commentaries], Grand Rapids: Zondervan, 1957.

*Longenecker, Richard N. *Galatians.* Dallas: Word, 1990.

*Lührmann, Dieter. *Galatians.* Minneapolis: Fortress, 1992.

Luther, Martin. *A Commentary on St. Paul's Epistle to the Galatians.* Grand Rapids: Zondervan, n.d. (From lectures delivered in 1531.)

*Matera, Frank J. *Galatians.* Sacra Pagina. Collegeville, MN: Michael Glazier, 1992.

Ridderbos, Herman. *The Epistle of Paul to the Churches of Galatia.* New International Commentary on the New Testament. Grand Rapids: Eerdmans, 1953.

Ephesians and Colossians (see also under Philippians and Philemon)

Abbott, T. K. *A Critical and Exegetical Commentary on the Epistles to the Ephesians and to the Colossians.* International Critical Commentary. Edinburgh: T. & T. Clark, 1897.

*Barth, Markus, and Blanke, Helmut. *Colossians.* Anchor Bible. New York: Doubleday, 1994.

*Barth, Markus. *Ephesians.* 2 vols. Anchor Bible. Garden City, NY: Doubleday, 1974.

Lightfoot, J. B. *Saint Paul's Epistles to the Colossians and to Philemon.* 6th ed. London: Macmillan, 1882.

*Lincoln, Andrew T. *Ephesians.* Word Biblical Commentary. Dallas: Word, 1990.

*Lincoln, Andrew T., and Wedderburn, A. J. M. *The Theology of the Later Pauline Letters.* New Testament Theology. Cambridge: Cambridge University Press, 1993.

Lohse, Eduard. *Colossians and Philemon.* Hermeneia: A Critical and Historical Commentary on the Bible. Philadelphia: Fortress, 1971.

*Martin, Ralph P. *Colossians and Philemon.* New Century Bible Commentary. Grand Rapids: Eerdmans, 1974.

*———. *Ephesians, Colossians, and Philemon.* Interpretation: A Bible Commentary for Teaching and Preaching. Louisville: Westminster/John Knox, 1991.

Mitton, C. Leslie. *Ephesians.* New Century Bible. London: Oliphants, 1976.

*Moule, C. F. D. *The Epistles of Paul the Apostle to the Colossians and to Philemon.* Cambridge Greek Testament Commentary. Cambridge: Cambridge University Press, 1957.

*O'Brien, Peter T. *Colossians, Philemon.* Word Biblical Commentary. Waco, TX: Word, 1982.

Pokorný, Petr. *Colossians: A Commentary.* Peabody, MA: Hendrickson, 1991.

Robinson, J. Armitage. *St. Paul's Epistle to the Ephesians.* London: Macmillan, 1922.

*Schnackenburg, Rudolf. *The Epistle to the Ephesians: A Commentary.* Edinburgh: T. & T. Clark, 1991.

*Schweizer, Eduard. *The Letter to the Colossians: A Commentary.* Minneapolis: Augsburg, 1982.

*Simpson, E. K., and Bruce, F. F. *Commentary on the Epistles to the Ephesians and Colossians.* New International Commentary on the New Testament. Grand Rapids: Eerdmans, 1957.

Thurston, Bonnie. *Reading Colossians, Ephesians, and 2 Thessalonians: A Literary and Theological Commentary.* New York: Crossroad, 1995.

Westcott, Brooke Foss. *Saint Paul's Epistle to the Ephesians.* London: Macmillan, 1906; reprint, Minneapolis: Klock & Klock, 1978.

Philippians and Philemon (See also under Ephesians and Colossians)

Beare, Francis Wright. *The Epistle to the Philippians.* Harper's New Testament Commentaries. New York: Harper & Row, 1959.

Caird, George B. *Paul's Letters from Prison: Ephesians, Philippians, Colossians, Philemon in the Revised Standard Version.* New Clarendon Bible. Oxford: Oxford University Press, 1976.

Collange, Jean-Francois. *The Epistle of Saint Paul to the Philippians.* London: Epworth, 1979.

*Craddock, Fred. *Philippians.* Interpretation: A Bible Commentary for Teaching and Preaching. Atlanta: John Knox, 1985.

*Fee, Gordon D. *Paul's Letter to the Philippians.* New International Commentary on the New Testament. Grand Rapids: Eerdmans, 1995.

*Hawthorne, Gerald. *Philippians.* Word Biblical Commentary. Waco, TX: Word, 1983.

Houlden, J. Leslie. *Paul's Letters from Prison: Philippians, Colossians, Philemon, and Ephesians.* Pelican New Testament Commentaries. London: SCM, 1977.

Knox, John. *Philemon among the Letters of Paul: A New view of its Place and Importance.* 2nd ed. New York: Abingdon, 1959.

*Lightfoot, Joseph Barber. *St. Paul's Epistle to the Philippians.* London: Macmillan, 1913; reprint [Zondervan Commentary], Grand Rapids: Zondervan, 1953.

*Martin, Ralph P. *Philippians.* New Century Bible Commentary. Grand Rapids: Eerdmans, 1980.

*O'Brien, Peter T. *Commentary on Philippians.* New International Greek Testament Commentary. Grand Rapids: Eerdmans, 1991.

*Petersen, Norman R. *Rediscovering Paul: Philemon and the Sociology of Paul's Narrative World.* Philadelphia: Fortress, 1985.

Plummer, Alfred. *A Commentary on St. Paul's Epistle to the Philippians.* London: R. Scott, 1919; reprint [Evangelical Masterworks], Old Tappan, NJ: Revell, 1981.

*Vincent, Marvin R. *A Critical and Exegetical Commentary on the Epistles to the Philippians and to Philemon.* International Critical Commentary. Edinburgh: T. & T. Clark, 1897.

*Witherington III, Ben C. *Friendship and Finances in Philippi: The Letter of Paul to the Philippians.* The New Testament in Context. Valley Forge, PA, 1995.

Thessalonian Epistles

Best, Ernest. *A Commentary on the First and Second Epistles to the Thessalonians.* Harper's New Testament Commentaries. New York: Harper & Row, 1972.

Bruce, F. F. *1 & 2 Thessalonians.* Word Biblical Commentary. Waco, TX: Word, 1982.

*Collins, Raymond F. *Studies on the First Letter to the Thessalonians.* Leuven: Leuven University Press, 1984.

*———, ed. *The Thessalonian Correspondence.* Bibliotheca Ephemeridum Theologicarum Louvaniensium, no. LXXXVII. Leuven: Leuven University Press, 1990.

Frame, James Everett. *A Critical and Exegetical Commentary on the Epistles of St. Paul to the Thessalonians.* International Critical Commentary. Edinburgh: T. & T. Clark, 1912.

*Jewett, Robert. *The Thessalonian Correspondence: Pauline Rhetoric and Millenarian Piety.* Foundations & Facets: New Testament. Philadelphia: Fortress, 1986.

Malherbe, Abraham. *Paul and the Thessalonians: The Philosophic Tradition of Pastoral Care.* Philadelphia: Fortress, 1987.

*Marshall, I. Howard. *1 and 2 Thessalonians.* New Century Bible Commentary. Grand Rapids: Eerdmans, 1983.

Milligan, George. *St. Paul's Epistles to the Thessalonians.* London: Macmillan, 1908; reprint [Evangelical Masterworks], Old Tappan, NJ: Revell, n.d.

*Morris, Leon. *The First and Second Epistles to the Thessalonians.* Rev. ed. New International Commentary on the New Testament. Grand Rapids: Eerdmans, 1991.

*Wanamaker, Charles A. *Commentary on 1 & 2 Thessalonians.* New International Greek Testament Commentary. Grand Rapids: Eerdmans, 1990.

Pastoral Epistles

*Barrett, C. K. *The Pastoral Epistles in the New English Bible.* New Clarendon Bible. Oxford: Clarendon, 1963.

Dibelius, Martin, and Conzelmann, Hans. *The Pastoral Epistles.* Hermeneia: A Critical and Historical Commentary on the Bible. Philadelphia: Fortress, 1972.

Fee, Gordon D. *Timothy, Titus.* New International Biblical Commentary. Peabody, MA: Hendrickson, 1989.

*Guthrie, Donald. *The Pastoral Epistles.* Tyndale New Testament Commentaries. Grand Rapids: Eerdmans, 1957.

*Hanson, A. T. *The Pastoral Epistles.* New Century Bible Commentary. Grand Rapids: Eerdmans, 1982.

*Houlden, J. L. *The Pastoral Epistles: I and II Timothy, Titus.* New Testament Commentaries. Philadelphia: Trinity, 1989.

*Kelly, J. N. D. *The Pastoral Epistles: Timothy I & II and Titus.* Harper's New Testament Commentaries. New York: Harper & Row, 1960.

*Knight III, George W. *Commentary on the Pastoral Epistles.* New International Greek Testament Commentary. Grand Rapids: Eerdmans, 1992.

Lock, Walter. *A Critical and Exegetical Commentary on the Pastoral Epistles.* International Critical Commentary. Edinburgh: T. & T. Clark, 1924.

*Oden, Thomas C. *First and Second Timothy and Titus.* Interpretation: A Bible Commentary for Teaching and Preaching. Atlanta: John Knox, 1989.

*Quinn, Jerome D., and Wacker, William C. *The First and Second Letters to Timothy.* Anchor Bible. New York: Doubleday, 1995.

*Quinn, Jerome D. *The Letter to Titus.* Anchor Bible. New York: Doubleday, 1990.

Verner, David C. *The Household of God: The Social World of the Pastoral Epistles.* Society of Biblical Literature Dissertation Series, no. 71. Chica, CA: Scholars, 1983.

*Young, Francis. *The Theology of the Pastoral Epistles.* New Testament Theology. Cambridge: Cambridge University Press, 1994.

Hebrews

*Attridge, Harold W. *Hebrews.* Hermeneia: A Critical and Historical Commentary on the Bible. Minneapolis: Fortress, 1989.

*Bruce, F. F. *The Epistle to the Hebrews.* New International Commentary on the New Testament. Grand Rapids: Eerdmans, 1964.

Buchanan, George Wesley. *To the Hebrews.* Anchor Bible. Garden City, NY: Doubleday, 1972.

Delitzsch, Franz. *Commentary on the Epistle to the Hebrews.* 2 vols. Edinburgh: T. & T. Clark. 1871; reprint, Minneapolis: Klock & Klock, 1978.

*Ellingworth, Paul. *Commentary on Hebrews.* New International Greek Testament Commentary. Grand Rapids: Eerdmans, 1993.

*Hughes, Philip Edgcumbe. *A Commentary on the Epistle to the Hebrews.* Grand Rapids: Eerdmans, 1977.

*Hurst, L. D. *The Epistle to the Hebrews: Its Background of Thought.* Society for New Testament Studies Monograph Series, no. 65. Cambridge: Cambridge University Press, 1990.

Käsemann, Ernst. *The Wandering People of God: An Investigation of the Letter to the Hebrews.* Minneapolis: Augsburg, 1984.

Kistemaker, Simon J. *Hebrews*. Grand Rapids: Baker, 1984.

*Lane, William L. *Hebrews: A Call to Commitment*. Peabody, MA: Hendrickson, 1985.

*——. *Hebrews 1-8*. Word Biblical Commentary. Dallas: Word, 1991.

*——. *Hebrews 9-13*. Word Biblical Commentary. Dallas: Word, 1991.

Lehne, Susanne. *The New Covenant in Hebrews*. Journal for the Study Supplement Series, no. 44. Sheffield: JSOT, 1990.

*Lindars, Barnabas. *The Theology of the Letter to the Hebrews*. New Testament Theology. Cambridge: Cambridge University Press, 1991.

Moffatt, James. *A Critical and Exegetical Commentary on the Epistle to the Hebrews*. International Critical Commentary. Edinburgh: T. & T. Clark, 1924.

Scholer, John M. *Proleptic Priests: Priesthood in the Epistle to the Hebrews*. Journal for the Study of the New Testament Supplement Series, no. 49. Shefffield: JSOT, 1991.

*Westcott, Brooke Foss. *The Epistle to the Hebrews: The Greek Text with Notes and Essays*. London: Macmillan, 1892; reprint, Grand Rapids: Eerdmans, 1974.

James (See also under Peter and Jude)

Adamson, James B. *The Epistle of James*. New International Commentary on the New Testament. Grand Rapids: Eerdmans, 1976.

——. *James: The Man and His Message*. Grand Rapids: Eerdmans, 1989.

*Davids, Peter. *The Epistle of James: A Commentary on the Greek Text*. New International Greek Testament Commentary. Grand Rapids: Eerdmans, 1982.

Dibelius, Martin. *James*. Revised by Heinrich Greeven. Hermeneia: A Critical and Historical Commentary on the Bible. Philadelphia: Fortress, 1975.

Hort, Fenton John Anthony. *The Epistle of St. James*. London: Macmillan, 1909.

*Johnson, Luke Timothy. *James*. Anchor Bible. New York: Doubleday, 1995.

*Laws, Sophie. *A Commentary on the Epistle of James*. Harper's New Testament Commentaries. San Francisco: Harper & Row, 1981.

*Martin, Ralph P. *James*. Word Biblical Commentary. Waco, TX: Word, 1988.

Mayor, Joseph B. *The Epistle of St. James: The Greek Text with Introduction, Notes, Comments and Further Studies in the Epistle of St. James*. 3rd ed. London: Macmillan, 1913; reprint, Minneapolis: Klock & Klock, 1977.

Mitton, C. Leslie. *The Epistle of James*. London: Marshall, Morgan and Scott, 1974.

Ropes, John H. *A Critical and Exegetical Commentary on the Epistle of St. James*. International Critical Commentary. Edinburgh: T. & T. Clark, 1916.

Petrine Epistles and Jude

*Bauckham, Richard J. *Jude and the Relatives of Jesus in the Early Church*. Edinburgh: T. & T. Clark, 1990.

*———. *Jude, 2 Peter*. Word Biblical Commentary. Waco, TX: Word, 1983.

Beare, Francis Wright. *The First Epistle of Peter: The Greek Text with Introduction and Notes*. 3rd ed. Oxford: Basil Blackwood, 1970.

Best, Ernest. *I Peter*. New Century Bible Commentary. Grand Rapids: Eerdmans, 1971.

Bigg, Charles. *A Critical and Exegetical Commentary on the Epistles of St. Peter and St. Jude.* International Critical Commentary. Edinburgh: T. & T. Clark, 1901.

*Chester, Andrew, and Martin, Ralph P. *The Theology of the Letters of James, Peter, and Jude.* New Testament Theology. Cambridge: Cambridge University Press, 1994.

Elliott, John H. *A Home for the Homeless: A Sociological Exegesis of I Peter, its Situation and Strategy.* Philadelphia: Fortress, 1981.

*Goppelt, Leonhard. *A Commentary on 1 Peter.* Grand Rapids: Eerdmans, 1993.

*Green, E. M. B. *The Second Epistle General of Peter and the General Epistle of Jude.* Tyndale New Testament Commentaries. Grand Rapids: Eerdmans, 1968.

Kelly, J. N. D. *A Commentary on the Epistles of Peter and of Jude.* Harper's New Testament Commentaries. New York: Harper & Row, 1969.

Luther, Martin. *Commentary on Peter & Jude.* Grand Rapids: Kregel, 1990. (Originally published, in German, in 1523 and 1539.)

*Mayor, Joseph B. *The Epistle of St. Jude and the Second Epistle of St. Peter: Greek Text with Introduction, Notes, and Comments.* London: Macmillan, 1907; reprint, Minneapolis: Klock & Klock, 1978.

*Michaels, J. Ramsey. *1 Peter.* Word Biblical Commentary. Waco, TX: Word, 1988.

*Neyrey, Jerome H. *2 Peter, Jude.* Anchor Bible. New York: Doubleday, 1993.

Perkins, Pheme. *First and Second Peter, James, and Jude.* Interpretation: A Bible Commentary for Teaching and Preaching. Louisville: Westminster/John Knox, 1995.

*Selwyn, Edward Gordon. *The First Epistle of St. Peter: The Greek Text with Introduction, Notes and Essays.* 2nd ed. London: Macmillan, 1947.

Talbert, Charles H., ed. *Perspectives on First Peter.* Special Studies Series, no. 9. Macon, GA: Mercer University Press, 1986.

*Watson, Duane Frederick. *Invention, Arrangement, and Style: Rhetorical Criticism of Jude and 2 Peter.* Society of Biblical Literature Dissertation Series, no. 104. Atlanta: Scholars, 1988.

Johannine Epistles

Brooke, A. E. *A Critical and Exegetical Commentary on the Johannine Epistles.* International Critical Commentary. Edinburgh: T. & T. Clark, 1912.

*Brown, Raymond E. *The Epistles of John.* Anchor Bible. Garden City, NY: Doubleday, 1982.

Bultmann, Rudolf. *The Johannine Epistles.* Hermeneia: A Critical and Historical Commentary on the Bible. Philadelphia: Fortress, 1973.

Dodd, C. H. *The Johannine Epistles.* Moffatt New Testament Commentary. London: Hodder and Stoughton, 1946.

Houlden, J. L. *A Commentary on the Johannine Epistles.* Harper's New Testament Commentaries. New York: Harper & Row, 1973.

Lieu, Judith. *The Second and Third Epistles of John.* Studies of the New Testament and its World. Edinburgh: T. & T. Clark, 1986.

*———. *The Theology of the Johannine Epistles.* New Testament Theology. Cambridge: Cambridge University Press, 1991.

*Marshall, I. Howard. *The Epistles of John.* New International Commentary on the New Testament. Grand Rapids: Eerdmans, 1978.

*Schnackenburg, Rudolf. *The Johannine Epistles: Introduction and Commentary.* New York: Crossroad, 1992.

*Smalley, Stephen S. *1,2,3 John.* Word Biblical Commentary. Waco, TX: Word, 1984.

Smith, D. Moody. *First, Second, and Third John.* Interpretation: A Bible Commentary for Teaching and Preaching. Louisville: Westminster/John Knox, 1991.

*Westcott, Brooke Foss. *The Epistles of St. John: The Greek Text, with Notes and Addenda.* London: Macmillan, 1883; reprint, Grand Rapids: Eerdmans, 1966.

Book of Revelation

*Bauckham, Richard J. *The Climax of Prophecy: Studies on the Book of Revelation.* Edinburgh: T. & T. Clark, 1993.

*———. *The Theology of the Book of Revelation.* New Testament Theology. Cambridge: Cambridge University Press, 1993.

*Beasley-Murray, George R. *The Book of Revelation.* New Century Bible Commentary. Grand Rapids: Eerdmans, 1981.

Boring, M. Eugene. *Revelation.* Interpretation: A Bible Commentary for Teaching and Preaching. Atlanta: John Knox, 1989.

*Caird, George B. *The Revelation of St. John the Divine.* Harper's New Testament Commentaries. New York: Harper & Row, 1966.

Charles, R. H. *A Critical and Exegetical Commentary on the Revelation of St. John.* 2 vols. International Critical Commentary. Edinburgh: T. & T. Clark, 1920.

Ellul, Jacques. *Apocalypse: The Book of Revelation.* New York: Seabury, 1977.

———. *The Meaning of the City.* Grand Rapids: Eerdmans, 1970.

Fiorenza, Elisabeth Schüssler. *The Book of Revelation: Justice and Judgment.* Philadelphia: Fortress, 1985.

Guthrie, Donald. *The Relevance of John's Apocalypse.* Grand Rapids: Eerdmans, 1987.

Harrington, Wilfrid J. *Revelation.* Sacra Pagina. Collegeville, MN: Michael Glazier, 1993.

König, Adrio. *The Eclipse of Christ in Eschatology.* Grand Rapids: Eerdmans, 1989.

*Ladd, George Eldon. *A Commentary on the Revelation of John.* Grand Rapids: Eerdmans, 1969.

*Mounce, Robert H. *The Book of Revelation.* New International Commentary on the New Testament. Grand Rapids: Eerdmans, 1977.

Mulholland, M. Robert, Jr. *Revelation: Holy Living in an Unholy World.* Grand Rapids: Zondervan, 1990.

Ramsey, William M. *The Letters to the Seven Churches of Asia.* Revised and updated by Mark W. Wilson. Peabody, MA: Hendrickson, 1994.

Roloff, Jürgen. *Revelation.* Minneapolis: Fortress, 1993.

Swete, Henry Barclay. *Commentary on Revelation: The Greek Text with Introduction, Notes and Indexes.* London: Macmillan, 1911; reprint, Grand Rapids: Kregel, 1977.

Wainwright, Arthur W. *Mysterious Apocalypse: Interpreting the Book of Revelation.* Nashville: Abingdon, 1993.

APPENDIX: Bible Software Programs

English Texts	KJV	RSV	NRSV	NIV	NASB	ASV	YLT	DBY	NKJV	TLB	NCV
AnyText	•	•	•	•							
Bible Master (DOS)	•	•	•	•	•						
BibleSource for Win.	•	•	•	•	•						
Bible Windows[1]	•	•	•			•					
BibleWorks for Win.	•	•	•	•	•	•			•		
*GRAMCORD (Win)[†]	•	•	•	•	•	•	•	•	•		
ACCORDANCE (Mac)	•	•	•	•		•					
Harvest PC Bible (Win)[2]	•	•	•	•		•			•	•	
The Holy Scriptures[3,4] (W/D)	•	•	•	•		•		•	•	•	
*Logos CD WordLibrary (Win)	•	•[6]	•[6]	•	•[6]	•			•[6]		
MacBible (Mac)[3]	•	•	•	•	•	•					
Online Bible (DOS)[5]	•	•	•	•		•	•	•	•		
PC Study Bible	•	•	•	•	•	•			•		
QuickVerse (W/D)	•	•	•	•	•	•			•	•	•
SeedMaster for Win.[1,7]	•	•	•	•	•[8]	•	•	•	•	•	•
Thompson Chain HyperBible (Win)	•	•	•	•	•				•	•	
Word Search for Win.[3]	•		•	•	•	•			•	•	

* Although these products were not yet ready for review at press time—data is based on manufacturer's claims—it is the reviewer's opinion, based upon previous versions of the software, they will be worthy of evaluation by potential users.

† GRAMCORD uses SeedMaster/Win as its "front end," therefore, it uses all the same resources as SeedMaster

[1] Will also read most Online Bible texts.
[2] Also available: New Jerusalem Vers.
[3] Also available: New American Bible

[4] Other available English versions include: Inspired Vers. and NRSV-Catholic Vers.
[5] Other available English versions include: Bible in Basic English; Modern KJV; Green's Literal Translation; Weymouth N.T.
[6] Not included in all versions.
[7] Also available: Today's English Vers., Concordant Literal Vers., International Children's Bible
[8] With embeded Strong's numbers.

Original Language Texts	UBS 3rd ed. / Nestle Aland 26 New Testament	Textus Receptus 1550/1891	Byzantine / Majority Text Form	Transliterated Greek N.T.	LXX Greek Old Testament	BHS Hebrew O.T.	Latin Vulgate Bible
AnyText	●				●[8]	●	●
BibleSource for Win.[1]	●[2]			●			
Bible Windows[3]	see footnote 7						
BibleWorks for Win.[3]	●[2]	●			●[8]	●	●
GRAMCORD (Win)[3] ACCORDANCE (Mac)[3]	●				●[8]	●	●
Logos CD WordLibrary (Win)[3]	●	●	●		●[8]	●[4]	●
MacBible (Mac)	●					●	
Online Bible (DOS)	see footnote 5	●[6]	●	●		see footnote 5	
SeedMaster for Win.	●	●			●	●	

NOTE: The following currently have no available original language texts: Bible Master, Thompson Chain HyperBible, Harvest PC Bible, Word Search for Windows.

NOTE: The following currently have only the transliterated Greek New Testament: The Holy Scriptures; PC Study Bible (Integration of original language material is planned for a future version.); QuickVerse

[1] Includes eclectic NIV version of the Greek NT
[2] Contains UBS4/NA27 text.
[3] Also included: Greek and Hebrew morphological databases.
[4] UBS Hebrew, not BHS.

[5] Also includes Westcott/Hort NT with variant readings of NA26; Hebrew Consonantal Text, similar to BHS. Greek & Hebrew displayed in VGA & EGA modes; extended ASCII used for CGA & monochrome. No diacritical marks, punctuation, accentuation, capitalization, breathing marks (Greek), vowel points (Heb.).
[6] Includes embeded parsing info and Strong's Numbers.
[7] Includes the Analytical Greek NT.
[8] Includes morphology.

English Resources	Embedded Strong's numbers[1]	Strong's Dict. (or equiv.)	Treas. of Scripture Know.	Nave's Topical Bible	Easton's Bible Dict.	Scofield Notes	Robertson's Word Pictures	People's N.T. Commentary
AnyText	●							
Bible Windows	●[2]							
BibleWorks for Win.	●		●	●	●		●	
GRAMCORD (Win)[3]								
Harvest PC Bible (Win)	●	●						
The Holy Scriptures (W/D)	●	●						
Logos CD WordLibrary (Win)[4,5,6]	●	●	●	●				
Online Bible (DOS)[6,7]	●	●	●	●	●	●		●
PC Study Bible[10,6]	●	●	●	●				
QuickVerse (W[8,9]/D)		●		●				
SeedMaster for Win.[8,6,7]	●	●	●	●	●	●	●	●
Thompson Chain HyperBible (Win)[4,7]								
Word Search for Win.[4]	●	●	●	●				

NOTE: These programs have none of these resources: BibleMaster, BibleSource for Windows, ACCORDANCE, MacBible

1 In KJV.
2 In Online Bible databases only
3 Only through integration with SeedMaster
4 Includes maps.
5 Includes the New Bible Dictionary, Harper's Bible Dictionary, Bible Knowledge Comment., Harper's Bible Comment., Jerome Biblical Comment.
6 Also available: Matt. Henry's Commentary
7 Available/Includes Thompson's Chain References
8 Add-on maps: Parsons PC Bible Atlas (Windows)
9 Add-on dictionary: Holman's Bible Dictionary
10 Add-on dictionary: Nelson's Bible Dictionary

Original Language Resources	Vine's Expository Dictionary	BDB-Gesenius' Hebrew Lexicon	Thayer's Greek-English Lexicon	UBS Greek NT Dictionary	Liddell & Scott's Intermediate Lexicon	Louw & Nida's Greek-English Lexicon
AnyText[1]						
BibleSource for Win[1]						
Bible Windows		(see footnote 2)		•	•	•
BibleWorks for Win.[3]		•	•			
GRAMCORD (Win)[4]						
ACCORDANCE (Mac)[1]						
Logos CD WordLibrary[3] (Win)	•				•	•
MacBible (Mac)[1]						
Online Bible (DOS)		•	•			
PC Study Bible	•[6]					
SeedMaster for Win.	•	•	•	•		

[1] No original language resources available at this time.
[2] Includes the "Simple Electronic Hebrew Glossary"
[3] Includes Friberg's Analytical Greek Lexicon
[4] All resources provided by SeedMaster/Win.
[5] Includes Abridged Kittel, BAGD Greek Lexicon, Chapman's Greek NT Insert.
[6] Includes dictionaries of both the Old and New Testaments.

Notable Features

	Notable Features
AnyText	This company's strong suit is in font design for many different languages.
Bible Master (DOS)	Use DOS? Like the NASB? Check out this program.
BibleSource for Win.	If your main study Bible is the NIV, this is a good choice.
Bible Windows	Louw & Nida's lexicon is a nice addition; Particularly good program for Greek work.
BibleWorks for Win.	This CD is a shining collection. Very advanced, but still easy, original language capabilities.
GRAMCORD (Win) ACCORDANCE (Mac)	The DOS predecessor of these programs has long been considered among the best Greek grammatical searching programs available. GRAMCORD: Very intimate integration with SeedMaster.
Harvest PC Bible (Win)	This is the exact same program as The Holy Scriptures for Windows.
The Holy Scriptures (W/D)	This is the exact same program as the Harvest PC Bible.
Logos CD WordLibrary (Win)	Available in four different "levels," whose contents vary by price/features.
MacBible (Mac)	Greek and Hebrew are available, but are not grammatically tagged. Very complete documentation.
Online Bible (DOS)	Individual texts/resources prices range $5 to $30 on diskette; CD is $20 and contains most diskette master files. Can print directly to Windows clipboard. Best price/performance ratio (CD) for DOS.
PC Study Bible	Personal notes feature not available; workspace cannot be saved; overall, a nice package.
QuickVerse (W/D)	Excellent integration of personal notes for words, verses, chapters, books.
SeedMaster for Win.	Best price/performance ratio for Windows. Can use GRAMCORD search engine; Parsons PC Bible Atlas. Four CD's available.
Thompson Chain HyperBible (Win)	Reviewed version only displays 640x480 resolution. Very non-standard Windows interface.
Word Search for Win.	This program takes a little getting used to, but it's worth the effort. "Desktop" metaphor very attractive.

Other good resources on Bible study software include:

Christian Computing Magazine
800-456-1868
http://www.website.net/~ccmag/

Church Bytes Magazine
919-490-8927
NEIL_HOUK.parti@ecunet.org

Shawn Abigail's *Bible Study Software FAQ* (updated monthly)
Available in the Usenet newsgroups:
soc.religion.christian.bible-study *and* soc.religion.christian.

INDEX